What You
Should Know About
SPIES AND SABOTEURS

What You
Should Know About
SPIES
AND SABOTEURS

BY

WILL IRWIN
and
THOMAS M. JOHNSON

W · W · NORTON & COMPANY · INC.
PUBLISHERS   NEW YORK

First Edition

PRINTED IN THE UNITED STATES OF AMERICA
FOR THE PUBLISHERS BY THE VAIL-BALLOU PRESS, INC.

FOREWORD

For most of the material on which we base this book we are indebted to men who are authorities on the subject. We would like to mention them and to thank them by name. But secret service, to be effective, must be anonymous, and to name them would be to do them a disservice. In order that the public may know, they have given us their time, the fruits of their accumulated experience, and their confidence. On our own behalf and that of our publisher we thank them most heartily. However, we can mention Mr. Ladislas Farago, who supplied some information embodied in Chapters Two and Four.

W. I. and T. M. J.

CONTENTS

LIST OF ILLUSTRATIONS

CHAPTER ONE

THE SECRETS OF SECRET
SERVICE

WORLD WAR II has increased beyond all precedent and expectation the scope of secret service. Napoleon said rightly that the intellectual and moral aspects of war were three times as important as the purely physical. Generals, admirals, and ministers of foreign affairs seem at last to have learned this lesson. No other war has seen so many spies, counterspies, saboteurs, intelligence officers, procurers of treason, and agents of propaganda actively at work; and in none other have these soldiers of underground warfare scored such notable results. Secret service on an unprecedented scale largely accounts for the collapse of Belgium, Holland, and France in 1940. Plain espionage made possible the crushing Japanese attack on Pearl Harbor in 1941. In the captive countries of Europe and the Orient, patriots by the millions are spying on their conquerors. Although the story cannot yet be told, expert naval intelligence laid the foundation for our notable victory off Midway Island in 1942; and a clash between German and American spies and counterspies preceded the amazingly successful North African landing of that year.

Like total war in general, secret service touches every life in a belligerent nation; and we are writing in order that the citizen may play his part—not necessarily in espionage, but in counterespionage against stealthy enemies in our midst. To do that intelligently, he must have knowledge.

Secret service is rightly named. When the war is over and the fighting done, generals write their memoirs, departments of operations open their records; but modern departments of intelligence, if they know their business, bottle up or destroy their archives. Although some directors of secret service live in history, many of the greatest individual spies died unhonored, unsung, and unknown except to their immediate superiors. They proved their greatness by not getting caught when they were at work and by keeping the professional law of secrecy after they retired. So to most minds a fascinating air of mystery seems to hang about their operations, and the novelists have not failed to take notice. Out of revelations of ex-spies but mostly out of their own imaginations, they have drawn a picture which is a source of innocent merriment to most intelligence officers and spyhunters.

This is among other things an attempt to make our thinking on the topic realistic. First, perhaps, we should describe how a system of military, naval, or diplomatic intelligence is organized. Notice that we use the word "intelligence." That, although allied with espionage, is not exactly the same thing; and we can best approach the subject by going back into history.

Espionage, the art of finding by secret means what the

enemy is doing or going to do, is as old as war and diplomacy—the scouts whom Moses sent into the Promised
Land, Delilah working the secrets out of strong but stupid Samson on behalf of the Philistines, Mithridates establishing government by spies in the Near East, Julius
Caesar constantly referring to his *exploratores* in his
memoirs, Sir Francis Walsingham helping to thrash the
King of Spain by uncovering the plans and strength of
the Armada. It seems, however, to have been a rudimentary, hit-and-miss process. In prewar diplomacy the foreign minister worked with a few trusted agents who
usually reported by word of mouth; in war the spy went
forth, made his way back to the general and told his story.

Generals and admirals appear occasionally to have set
aside an officer to manage the spies, but organization of
the work under the specialists whom we know as intelligence officers did not appear on the scene until about the
period of our own Revolutionary War. Then we find
Lord Suffolk and William Eden in London managing
that diplomatic secret service whose agent Edward Ban-
croft completely fooled Benjamin Franklin, and the ill-
fated Major John André at British headquarters in New
York in control of military espionage against the Colonial
Army. In 1775, Washington laid the foundation of our
own intelligence service. One of his early memoranda
reads: "To 333⅓ dollars given to [————] to induce him
to go into the town of Boston to establish a secret correspondence for the purpose of conveying intelligence of
the enemy's movements and designs." After the failure
and execution of the heroic but inexpert Nathan Hale,

Washington perceived the necessity for keen professional work and appointed Major Benjamin Tallmadge to organize and direct it; history records that he did a good job.

Presently, the intelligence officer became an integral part of European army organization. But by 1861 we Americans seemed to have forgotten the lesson of the Revolution. Though the South had notable spies, some of whom like Belle Boyd live in song and story, it never created a real department of intelligence for its armies; these agents merely reported to President Davis, the Secretary of War, or to whatever general might have use for the information. The North made the initial mistake of selecting Allan Pinkerton as chief of secret service. An expert detective in civilian life, he and his employers learned that military intelligence is quite another matter. For instance: In 1862, Pinkerton reported that General Joseph Johnston had 200,000 men defending Richmond—thus causing McClellan to hesitate fatally in his advance up the peninsula—whereas the actual force was only about 80,000. Colonel Lafayette C. Baker, who had served as a spy in the field, took over and did better; but his work, which embraced both espionage and spyhunting, was poorly organized—else Lincoln might have lived on. On the other hand Major General Grenville M. Dodge early took control of intelligence for the Western armies and systematized the work so well as to foreshadow modern methods.

Meantime the Europeans, keeping the peace by balance of power and sitting always on a volcano, had begun to maintain organized intelligence work in the intervals between wars. Germany, always fascinated by the bright sword of Odin, took the lead—and has retained it ever since. During the preliminaries to the Austro-Prussian War of 1866 and the Franco-Prussian War of 1870, Wilhelm Stieber, perhaps the greatest spymaster of all time, rose to an importance second only to that of Bismarck. Stieber was a curious, crooked genius, as great spies not infrequently are. Born "lower middle class," into a snobbish, stratified society—the well-born Bismarck would offer him only his own left hand—a complex of inferiority akin to Hitler's drove him on to advance himself by any means, however sordid. He is suspected of having double-crossed even Prussia. He learned the practical side of his trade as a police official and as a roving spy in Austria, where he disguised himself as a peddler selling religious images—with obscene pictures for a side line. As Prussia awaited "the day" for dealing with Napoleon III, he created in France a forebear of the modern fifth column. His web of agents overlaid every grade of society from the Court to the village *estaminet*. Many of these agents were Frenchmen who had sold themselves for money; others, fashionable courtesans; still others, neutrals or Germans who had settled in France years before and were more or less assimilated into the population. With Teutonic thoroughness, Stieber's agents pried into every feature of the French Army—its proposed tactics, its scheme of strategy, the strengths and weaknesses of its high officers, its equipment, the good and bad points of its rifles, machine guns, artillery, and transport. On the eve of war, Napoleon's Minister of War reported that his army was ready "to the last gaiter-button." He might have added, with more truth, that Prussia knew that army to the last loose gaiter-button.

But Stieber did more than that. He organized, he virtually created, that modern military intelligence of which espionage is only a department. Back at the headquarters of the General Staff sat a body of expert officers, some of whom had served as spies in their time. It was their duty to take all this information, estimate the truth in each item, match this with that until they established a vital fact which they passed on to the Kaiser's generals or diplomats. When the war opened, intelligence officers at the front systematically questioned prisoners and civilians and sent the information to headquarters, where the experts gave it meaning. The Prussians knew that the French had clamped a censorship onto the press, but suspected that incompetence and an itch for glory would spatter it with flaws. So they established at Rome a sub-bureau of intelligence whose sole job was to comb the French newspapers and the stories of foreign war correspondents for details bearing on the movements and intentions of the French Army.

The idea was not entirely original; Confederates and Federals in our Civil War had watched the enemy newspapers closely for indiscreet items. But the systematic and complete gathering of such information was decidedly new. History records that on the seventh day after mobilization, German intelligence informed Field Marshal von Moltke on the position of every French army corps, and that a newspaper clipping, co-ordinated with other items from the French and foreign press, gave the information by means of which he so easily bottled up Marshal Bazaine's army at Metz.

Hitherto, the spy had been not only the backbone of intelligence work; he had been the whole skeleton. The gathering of information on the prospective or present enemy had been a kind of art; and Stieber and his assistants transferred it, partially at least, to the field of science, which works patiently from known facts to probable conclusions.

The modern spy is usually a searcher for small details, a picker-up of unconsidered trifles, many of which he may not himself understand. The harvest is being gathered at the other end of his line of communications, where an officer-specialist works at an intellectual task that resembles the assembling of a jigsaw puzzle. One piece of information comes from divisional intelligence officers who have been questioning prisoners at the front or going through the clothing of the dead for letters and diaries; another from a bit of atmospheric writing, missed by the censors, in a foreign newspaper; still another from the filed reports of a military or naval attaché stationed in the enemy capital before the war; and still another from an intercepted radio dispatch. All this, perhaps, before he takes notice of the information from his own spies. Sometimes a seemingly trivial item is the very thing he needs to complete the picture; which is the sound reason why armies censor so carefully all letters from the front, why governments ask or command their civilians and soldiers to padlock their tongues.

That method was Stieber's bequest to Europe. Although the spy was no longer the whole skeleton, he still remained the backbone of the system. Stieber had proved the value of continuous espionage in peace as well as in war. From the end of the Franco-Prussian War to the pistol shot that sounded World War I, Europe hopped with spies—businessmen established for the purpose near some center of military operations, serious-minded intelligence officers posing as commercial travelers, couriers, travel agents, hotel managers, traitors in general staffs, waiters and chambermaids in restaurants and cafés that officers and diplomats frequented, playboys, high courtesans, low prostitutes, habitual criminals.

Their operations bred a school of fiction and drama distinguished more for action than for accuracy of detail. There even grew up between nations a set of unwritten conventions concerning their conduct—a kind of left-handed code of ethics. Once, as in Elizabethan England, ambassadors frankly employed spies and smuggled the reports back to their kings. Now, sealed diplomatic bags went back and forth on the tacit assumption that diplomacy had divorced itself from espionage. Ambassadors, ministers, sometimes even military and naval attachés, took pains not to know what the intelligence departments were doing. Many of the spies worked alone, even as they do today. The penalty of discovery was death in time of war and a prison term in time of peace; but the captured spy might expect no defense, no recognition whatever, from his ambassador or his government. They repudiated him, denied him, even when he was innocent. When Captain Alfred Dreyfus was sent to Devil's Island for life on a charge of treason and espionage, the German Government knew perfectly that France had condemned the wrong man and could have saved him at any time; but Germany held her peace.

So on to World War I, wherein the scope of warfare spread to embrace nearly every activity of the national life, and the scope of secret service kept pace. The spy no longer confined his dark operations to armies. He pried into the operations of factories and laboratories; he studied the enemy sources of raw materials; for the benefit of that new horror, the submarine, he reported on the sailings and routes of naval vessels; he watched closely the morale of the civilian population. Also, there arose new classes of secret agents, notably saboteurs and propagandists.

Another world upheaval still greater in scope brought total war, and with it total espionage. During the truce of 1918–39 came the beginnings of the fifth column, a combination of spies, potential saboteurs, procured traitors, and subtle propagandists designed to weaken the enemy nation before war and to baffle its military effort when the war began. In all this, Germany led, as since the 1860's she has led all movements to intensify warfare; indeed total espionage is merely the revival and perfection of Frederick the Great's foreign policy. And espionage has always been the heart of Japanese diplomacy.

We must delimit a work of this length. Espionage is a kind of negative force. It does not act directly like sabotage, nor inspire action on the one hand and depress it on the other like propaganda. It only lights the way toward effective action. But the saboteur, at this stage of his development, behaves much like the spy. Often, indeed, the same man practices or directs both trades, whereas propaganda, a vastly intricate thing, stands somewhat apart. So ignoring those who dim the light, we shall confine ourselves to those who walk in darkness —the saboteur and the spy.

The exposure and conviction of the Duquesne and Ludwig rings in 1940 and 1942 and the case of the eight saboteurs in 1942 shocked the country into realizing that spies are working in our midst and that they are dangerous. It is not entirely a new experience for us; we had a primary lesson in the 1910's. But in the ensuing quarter-century of peace and isolation, we had forgotten it; and our thinking, guided by imaginative novelists, had become unrealistic.

On the eve of General Eisenhower's secret attack on North Africa, a woman stood on a New York dock watching workmen load boxes. Their labels clearly indicated their destination. A watchman strolled by.

"Why do you let me stay here?" she asked him. "I may be a spy, you know."

"Well, lady," he replied, "you don't look like a spy!"

He had in his mind some definite picture. A slithering, sinuous blonde perhaps, with allure in her eye and the

wickedness in her heart showing through the lines of her
sophisticated face—which leads up to the first lesson:
above all things, the spy must be inconspicuous. He must
blend with his environment like a commando trooper.
Actually, the fact that the lady did not look like a spy
tended to indicate that she might be one. The dramatic,
exhibitionist type is no longer wanted; Mata Hari was
the last of that species. Among the German mistakes in
the affair of the eight saboteurs was that of sending over
a man so conspicuous of face and form as tall, wolf-faced
George John Dasch. Four of them, landing on Long Island from a rubber boat, ran into coastguardsman John
C. Cullen. When, having received belated notice, the
F.B.I. arrived, these men had a start of eight hours. But
Cullen could describe this conspicuous leader of the
party; so could the station agent at Amagansett, where
they took a train for New York, and the trainmen. With
little difficulty, the F.B.I. picked him up in Yorkville.

Exaggerated disguises and false whiskers are emphati-
cally "out" of modern secret service. No longer does a
spy make himself up as, let us say, a physician. He *is* a
physician, complete with a genuine degree, genuine office and patients. It is an axiom of today's spymasters that
"if an agent has a 'cover,' it must be not phony, but the
real thing."

As for the life of a spy, it is much more often monotonous than adventurous. Even danger, when it lasts too
long, becomes a bore. The spy of fiction or the movies
usually sets forth to do one definite and important job
like stealing and copying the enemy's plan of campaign

or obtaining the design of a new weapon. That happens in real life, though rarely. The Dreyfus case turned on an attempt to get information about a new French field gun. Of late, we have exposed and foiled the German attempt to steal a specimen of our aerial bomb sight; and when naval Lieutenant Commander Farnsworth betrayed us to the Japanese, the navy had to change its scheme of battle tactics. But where one spy accomplishes such spectacular and complete results, ten thousand lonely, ill-paid men and women work at tasks that are no more interesting or rewarding than keeping accounts or selling brushes from door to door.

With one difference: the haunting sense of danger. For every spy there are myriad counterspies—policemen, agents of enemy intelligence, suspicious private citizens. He is even in danger from his own kind. An incompetent or double-crossing spy may ruin the most carefully laid plot. Therefore many intelligence departments keep spies on their own spies. And some of the continental Europeans, with whom this game is older and more ruthless than with the British and Americans, do not hesitate to make away with a spy who has proved himself indiscreet or faithless—sometimes by plain murder, more often by betraying him to the enemy through a premeditatedly careless message, a tip from some go-between, or an anonymous letter. As a subtle variation, sometimes, by way of deceiving the enemy, the procurers of his death arrange to load his person or lodgings with fake information!

CHAPTER TWO

THE SPY: WHO AND WHAT HE IS

INDIVIDUAL spies in time of war or preparation for war fall roughly into four classes: officers, patriotic volunteers, mercenaries, and informers.

The first, and in the past by far the most important, consists of professional army and navy officers who have undertaken this job in the spirit of "service in excess of duty." Not only are they cool, brave, and trained but they know what to look for and where to look—a most important point. Even an unusually observant civilian sent to report on the layout of a fortress would be like a husband sent to a reception by his wife with orders to describe Mrs. Fashion's dress and hat so that she might duplicate them. He would miss dozens of salient features. Officers serving as spies abroad are frequently commanders, not individual operators. They procure minor spies, either traitors, people of their own nationality resident in the foreign country, or neutrals, and after instructing them on what to look for organize the work and arrange means of communication. Sometimes officer-spies take actual and personal command of an expedition involving many subordinates. Clad in greasy overalls and battered sou'westers, Japanese naval officers served as supercargoes of the alleged fishing boats that used to snoop around our Pacific fleet during maneuvers, those crews of seal pirates that explored and sounded the outer Aleutian Islands in preparation for the landing of 1942.

Occasionally, there arises a situation so important and peculiar that only an officer can handle it. Such was the expedition of Lieutenant General Mark W. Clark to make contact and arrangements with the Free French patriots of North Africa before we landed our expeditionary force. No civilian could have done the job. Yet technically speaking, he and his party worked as spies. Had they been caught, the Vichy French could have done no less than jail them, and the Nazis might have shot or beheaded them. Incidentally, this exploit proves that intelligence work can still be romantic.

By universal custom, the officer-spy is seldom or never drafted for this work. He must volunteer. By a curious quirk of the military mind, a few professional officers still look down upon espionage, as did Robert E. Lee. Some of this rises from subconscious jealousy. The officer of the line likes to think that victories are due solely to his own brains and the valor of his men. And some of it is mere military conservatism. On the European continent, military men generally regard the patriot-spy, who works alone in constant danger of a knife in his back or a rope around his throat, as a greater hero than the soldier who fights in the open with his comrades beside him. As indeed he is. When we and the British raised monuments to Nathan Hale and Edith Cavell, tacitly we acknowledged

that inescapable fact. The Japanese, too, recognize un-
mercenary espionage for what it is—a supreme test of
courage, worthy of supreme honors.

The second class of spies consists of amateurs or semi-
amateurs—in some situations, especially during the preliminaries to war, almost as valuable as the officers. These
are men and women who volunteer for patriotic motives,
spiced perhaps with a yearning for adventure. English-
men of the leisure class traveling abroad used to "plug
for the Foreign Office" by watching diplomatic, social,
and commercial tendencies in the lands they visited; if
they chanced to pick up bits of military information, so
much the better. As often as not modern explorers were
also mapmakers. German-Americans who still loved the
old country imparted information when they revisited
it; and on all the six continents, transplanted Germans
spied on military activities in their lands of adoption.
The famous Count Luckner, cruising through the East
Indies a few years before the current war, planted spy
radio stations at strategic points. The office of the Hamburg American Steamship Line in New York was a nerve
center for espionage and sabotage during our period of
neutrality in World War I; the German Tourist Bureau
in New York and several Axis lines played the same game
with us between 1933 and 1941. The men who managed
all this were officials of the steamship companies, organizing espionage "on the side" while drawing salaries in
their regular positions. Often they were German reserve
officers. Among the Germans interned by us as enemy
aliens in 1942 were several technicians, good men at their

jobs, who until the cleanup by the F.B.I. worked in munitions factories and even government offices. Probably most of them had done no harm to us as yet. They were waiting for "the day" when they could make themselves useful.

As for the Japanese, the civilian was in peacetime the backbone of military and naval intelligence directed against us. For nearly a quarter of a century, the "gentleman's agreement" admitted one hundred Japanese a year to this country. Long before the Nazis originated the term, Japan had a totalitarian government. Japanese officials selected the favored immigrants. "The cement of her society is fear," said Helen Hyde, American painter, after fifteen years' residence in Japan. Before they sailed, agents of intelligence—military and especially naval— showed them their duty to the Mikado and the Empire. Most of them, probably, needed no persuasion or compulsion since nationalism is literally, not figuratively, a religion in Japan. Furthermore, the Mikado's army and navy drafted into service merchants and students entering on visitors' permits—no espionage, no passport; which introduces one advantage of the totalitarian government in this business of espionage and sabotage.

In spirit, and often in fact, they have supplanted the religion of God with the religion of the state. And "the state has no morals." No sense of good faith between man and man, no inherent human scruples may stand between the Nazi and his duty to Fatherland and Führer. Children must—and do—spy on parents suspected of dangerous thoughts; brother gives up brother to the

Gestapo; lying, snooping, blackmail, even murder, became consecrated acts when committed in the service of Moloch. The young Nazi miseducated in the state schools has lived in an atmosphere of watchfulness, intrigue, and deceit. The ordinary, decent American, Briton, or Scandinavian who for patriotic reasons volunteers as a spy must adjust himself to a world whose customs and practices differ but little from those of a criminal gang. Some of the things his country calls on him to do are not "cricket" or "playing ball" in his private code of ethics. Yet he must compete with Germans or Japanese, to whom the moral atmosphere of espionage is only a slight change from that of peace in their native lands.

The third class, in the past the largest one, consists of mercenaries serving solely for pay—combined, in many cases, with a perverted enjoyment of dangerous adventure. Generally speaking, they are the small spies, the mere privates. Sheer traitors—failures of civilian life who cannot resist the offer of money—have in all ages formed a large part of this class. Others have an old grievance against their own governments, as in the case of cashiered officers; others are morbid political dissenters; still others sheer criminals, loose ladies, common prostitutes. This system sinks to its depths in the case of opium addicts. Probably few normal people know the truth about the opium habit. When it is fully established the addict's mind and nerves are normal, or comparatively so, while the narcotic is in him. When he misses his daily dose of morphine, heroin, or hop, he falls into a mental, physical, and nervous hell. Opium for nonmedical purposes is expensive and in most countries hard to get. That, and not anything in the effects of the drug, is why so many "dope fiends" turn criminal. German and Japanese espionage and the illicit trade in opium have linked tentacles all over the world. The spy procurer promises his recruit not only wages but a regular and certain supply of the drug. If it stops, he faces unspeakable agony. Furthermore, in the case of the drug addicts, the criminals, and the other morally uncertain spies, the spymaster often holds a most potent threat. He has documentary evidence of their treason in his hands and can by devious means betray them to their own country's counterintelligence.

Purely as collectors of information, the professional officers constitute the most reliable class of spies; and the patriotic volunteers are not far behind. But the hirelings, being often unreliable human beings, behave as such. As Colonel Walther Nicolai, German spymaster, has said, the great embarrassment in secret service is the fact that you must often employ slippery people in conditions wherein you cannot watch them. A certain proportion of them will sell out to the enemy and send in artistically misleading reports. For a small example, in 1918 the Germans put a spy into the office of our Committee on Public Information in Switzerland. His job was to steal or copy documents, for which service Germany paid him twenty-five dollars a week. We were paying him fifty dollars a week to transmit to the Germans documents of our choice, which were composed to fool their readers. Other mercenaries exaggerate trifles by way of proving their

own value. Still others soldier on the job. A stock trick is
to digest nonsecret information from technical journals
and send it in as having come from "confidential sources."
Sometimes they assert that they have bought such stuff,
which enables them to pad their expense accounts. In
Madrid during 1917, small, mercenary spies for the Germans and the Allies used to meet at a certain café where
they traded information; and the same easy way of living
thrives today in the cafés of Switzerland and Portugal.
This immorality of the underlings is one reason why the
ideal intelligence officer must be a man of sterling character, able to distinguish the lie he is living from the
truth for which he is striving. If he lowers his personal
standards, decay will work upward from the bottom of
the structure.

What does the mercenary spy get out of it? Usually
relatively little; the average pickpocket probably does
better and with less risk. Certain German spies caught in
this country before Pearl Harbor rated salaries of two
hundred dollars a month and expenses—when they got
it. Transmission of money for the payroll is a surreptitious process, and the enemy is forever cutting the line. In
countries of lower living standards, the spy receives even
less. The $178,000 which the eight saboteurs buried and
the F.B.I. recovered is an illusory yardstick. This sum
was supposed to be split into bribes, salaries, and expense
accounts for a horde of saboteurs and couriers, for traveling expenses and incidentals. Occasionally a mercenary
who is also a boss does better. We have a record of $25,000
having been paid in one lump to Fritz Duquesne who is

a cross between a mercenary and an adventurer. It would be interesting to know how much of it stuck to his fingers.

The fourth class, the informers, are usually not spies in the popular sense of the word; yet they are often the most valuable of all. These are nationals of the country on which one is spying, who in their motives vary from idealists wishing to promote revolution to greedy persons distinguishable only from mercenary spies by the amount of their pay or, baldly, their bribe. Although they do piecework, the price generally comes high. The commonest members of this class are government officials, ranging from diplomats or staff officers down to filing clerks. During World War I, a German diplomat in a neutral country furnished our intelligence valuable information and did it free—he was trying to promote a republican revolution. After we entered the war, several other German officials came through, some of them for large bribes. If you can bribe a high official and make sure that he is being dishonestly honest with you, then you've got something! But a mere clerk or scrubwoman with access to confidential files may be almost as useful.

This is a war not only between nations but between ideologies. In the Axis nations secret communists or liberals are serving the United Nations as voluntary informers, just as secret fascists in the United Nations are serving Hitler and Mussolini. As there are more spies in the world now than ever before, so are there more informers.

One might add another class, small and overadvertised: the sheer adventurers. These people usually have a streak of exhibitionism in them and between jobs cannot restrain the impulse to confide their past adventures to the press. Fritz Duquesne, anti-British spy in the Boer War and both World Wars, is a specimen of this species. He seemed to have only one sincere spot in his twisted psychology: hatred for England. Otherwise he was a trickster, a boaster, a pathological liar. His last spy ring, assembled in the United States before Pearl Harbor, violated a cardinal principle in that practically every member knew every other member as a spy. Catch one and get him talking, and you had them all. It is probable that Duquesne did his cause more harm than good. He is now in prison under sentences amounting practically to a life term. Not all the simon-pure adventurers are so bad at their trade; some have done good work in brilliant flashes. But intelligence officers regard them as uncertain and unreliable.

There are other classifications such as "fixed-post" spies, "traveling" spies and couriers. Their titles, however, describe them. Also, women in espionage deserve separate mention. Sir Basil Thomson of Scotland Yard declared that if he had his way he would never employ women: "They do not make good spies, though married men may not believe it!" The continental European nations disagree. The advantage of woman spies lies in the "personal touch" on which all their sex are specialists. Prostitutes high and low and other ladies of easy virtue fill most pages of the old story. Anyone who has read spy fiction knows how they proceed—work the officer, statesman, or private in the ranks into the sentimental mood, during which he rests his weary head on your shoulder and blabs confidences; when you find an especially important victim, get him so enamored that he will betray his country for your sake. In this respect the novelists have not exaggerated very much. This process is going on all over the world today—blowsy beer-jerkers in Central American dives pumping half-drunken sailors; casually met girls in European or African cafés playing for soldiers; high *demimondaines* in Portuguese, Spanish, or French salons worming their way into the hearts of staff officers.

Even the patriotic woman spy, a world away from these people in personal morals, has sex in her favor. Sometimes the appeal of girlish helplessness works as well with a gallant man as does raw sex. The couriers whom E. V. Voska, director of Czechoslovakian counterespionage in the United States from 1914 to 1916, sent through enemy territory to Bohemia were all women of impeccably correct life; yet most of them, like Anna Chaloupkova to whom a monument stood in Prague before the Germans came, used to great advantage the "poor little girl" sentiment in man. So perhaps did even those outstanding feminine spies who depended on their brains, like the American Marguerite Harrison of World War I, France's Louise de Bettignies, and some of Britain's agents in the Near East.

Others capitalize their very lack of charm, their mouse-like quality. One of the greatest American spies of past wars was the spinster Elizabeth van Lew, an abolitionist Southerner who all through the Civil War sent to Washington, using her own manumitted slaves as assistants and couriers, invaluable data—military, diplomatic, and economic—on the state of the Southern Confederacy. Personally, she was a woman whom no man would turn to look at. But she had high social position; the military and political leaders of the Confederacy flocked to her receptions and in the supposed secrecy of her house unbosomed themselves. Although she had never received any instruction, she had an instinct for distinguishing between the important and the trivial. She invented her own ciphers and codes; and she concealed her operations so perfectly that her story did not come out until two generations after the Confederacy fell.

The aversion to women as spies applies especially to those of the *demimondaine* class, commonly used by the Japanese and the Continental nations and little or not at all by the British and Americans. They have a way of falling in love with their victims and joining the enemy; also, being moral defectives, they may sell out. The spymasters have felt that women in general lacked "feel" for a game so masculine as war, and, especially in this country, knowledge of its technique. However, the quarter-century since World War I has witnessed woman's emancipation in the Western nations. They have entered the man's world by the millions and are competing with him on his own terms. When the secret history of the second World War comes out, we are likely to find that the woman of character and brains like Marguerite Harrison or Elizabeth van Lew, rather than the harlot like Mata Hari, is the typical woman spy of these times.

How are civilian spies recruited? Most commonly, per-

haps, by an expert intelligence officer who, when war becomes imminent, visits the country of the prospective
enemy in the guise of a business or professional man.
Probably he brings along a few assistants whom he places
on "fixed post"—like a bartender in a water-front bar or
tavern frequented by sailors or navy-yard workers. He
keeps his ears and eyes open until they perceive a prospect. There follow subtle approaches and quiet investiga-
tions, before the agent assures himself that the embryo
spy is "right" and makes his proposition. This same agent
gives him such instruction as he needs, arranges for transmission of his messages, sets him to work, and serves as
paymaster. Informers especially are recruited by threat
of exposure of some secret vice or crime.

A typical recruiting and directing agent was Captain
Ulrich von der Osten who operated in New York before
we entered World War II. A fatal accident revealed his
operations and his system. When a taxicab killed him in
Times Square, a companion grabbed Osten's portfolio
and lost himself in the crowd. Witnesses reported this
odd circumstance to the police, who found the room
where he lived as "Señor Lido" containing some notes
and documents smelling of espionage. Investigation
proved that a so-called ring was already established here,
its head being Kurt Frederick Ludwig, American by
birth, German by education. He had recruited his small
band of assistants, including Lucy Boehmler and Helen
Pauline Mayer, from the Bund or its sympathizers.
Osten, but lately arrived, had come to take general charge
and to hunt new recruits.

Ludwig, afterward caught and convicted, had lived in the United States between 1925 and 1933, had returned in 1942 perfectly educated in espionage, ready to work efficiently. Probably he and his assistants did us more harm than the government admits. Incidentally, as evidence of the shift in woman spies from the sexual type to the cerebral, Mrs. Mayer had memorized all salient details of our new Flying Fortresses—a difficult feat for even an expert mechanic—and when arrested was preparing to sail to Japan to transmit the information without benefit of notes and drawings. And close to the chief sat Dr. Paul T. Borchart, once a major in the German Army, who assembled the data and gave them meaning before transmitting them in tabloid form to Germany.

During the first year of World War I, the German and Austrian governments secretly broke the old rules of diplomatic etiquette. The change first became apparent in the United States. Hitherto, military and naval attachés in foreign capitals were supposed to keep the skirts of their dress uniforms clean of espionage, to transmit only such information as their hosts chose to give them. But presently the Czechoslovakian counterspies of E. V. Voska and our own secret services learned that Captain Boy-Ed, German naval attaché at Washington, and Major von Papen, German military attaché, were up to their necks in the business of espionage and sabotage. Similarly, the consuls were supposed to limit their reports to matters of commerce, education, and the like. But now, the Austro-Hungarian consulate in New York became the general clearinghouse for Teutonic spies and saboteurs; and the consulates of the Central Powers in the other great American cities followed suit.

When the Nazis came into power, Germany abandoned diplomatic etiquette. Between September, 1939, and December, 1941, their consular corps in key cities like New York, Chicago, and San Francisco increased threefold. Every insider knew what the excess employees were doing. With the Japanese, diplomatic etiquette was always a mere pretense. The German consulates recruited their staffs from the reservoir of the Bund and from natives of lands where there were factions favorable to the Axis; the Japanese largely from the Japanese population already in the United States. However, the Oriental spy in a white man's land has the disadvantage of being conspicuous. So long as they confined themselves to the Japanese nationals already planted in this fertile field, they could go only so far, in spite of the fact that our ingenuous good nature had permitted them fully to photograph our military works, including the defenses of Pearl Harbor and the Panama Canal, to sound the approaches to our harbors, and to learn more about the remote Aleutians than we knew ourselves. They needed Caucasian aid.

Probably the Japanese consulates and intelligence officers had little hunting to do. In the two or three years before Pearl Harbor, the Germans were helping out by furnishing recruits from the Nazi element in this country. Also, a class of raffish international adventurers, of embarrassed wasters who will do anything for money, haunts all the world's metropolitan cities. Many of them have served as soldiers or as spies, if not for governments then for private interests; some among them have lived by crimes, like blackmail, in the intervals between jobs. The news that the Japanese were recruiting spies ran through this circle like mercury. The Japanese consular officials listened, smiling, to the sales talks of the applicants, and drew air in reverse through their teeth as they replied that the consulate was interested only in maintaining honorable and pleasant relations with the United States. But they put shadows upon the more promising of the applicants. For those who passed scrutiny, there followed a meeting, casually arranged or by appointment, in some park or remote roadhouse.

John S. Farnsworth, once a lieutenant commander in the United States Navy, stood in urgent need of money. He had acquired a few really important facts and documents concerning the construction of our naval vessels and our proposed tactics in case of war, and had been trying to sell them to foreign governments. He had no luck until he approached Commander Tachibana, of the Japanese naval intelligence, paymaster for spies on the West coast. It was arranged that Torachi Kono, a spy planted in Los Angeles long before, should bring Farnsworth his pay and arrange contact with another Japanese when he traveled to Hawaii to look into the defenses of Pearl Harbor. Happily for us, Farnsworth also met another man, professedly a Japanese spy but actually an agent for American counterespionage. Exit Farnsworth to a long term in prison.

Harry Thomas Thompson, once yeoman in the United

States Navy, now a convict serving a fifteen-year term, was a "volunteer." He made his first contact with the Japanese consulate at Los Angeles and his second with the embassy at Washington; and Lieutenant Commander Toshio Miyazaki, camouflaged as a language student at Stanford University, became his immediate superior. When Karl Allen Drummond, inspector in a military aircraft factory at Los Angeles, offered to betray his country, he was so eager to sell out that the Japanese thought he might be an agent of American espionage! They never put him on regular salary, but only bought from time to time blueprints and photographs stolen from his shop.

In Hawaii, the Japanese used peculiar but effective tactics. Probably they had always maintained a few spies among their transplanted fellow countrymen. But when they began to lay the plot for the Pearl Harbor outrage, they worked almost solely through their own Japanese consulate. The personnel of this office trebled during 1940–41; and the excess employees were all trained spies. By cable and wireless messages in cipher and code—which a stupid federal law prevented our counterespionage from intercepting—and by couriers on merchant vessels, these expert agents laid bare to the Japanese Navy all details of our defenses. They even gathered information on the habits of our defenders, including the fatal custom of granting generous leave on Saturday nights. When the carrier force prepared to attack, their information was a few days old. It was not, as generally believed, a wireless message that brought it up to date by revealing to them the anchorage of every ship in Pearl Harbor; it was a two-man Japanese submarine. Sneaking into the harbor, this marine scout took a look through the periscope, put back to sea and wirelessed the anchorages of our ships to the oncoming Japanese carriers.

Japan reaped a tragically abundant harvest for her pains. But another feature of her espionage has attracted less attention. For months after Pearl Harbor and our declaration of war, the Japanese tortured the imprisoned American newspaper correspondents to make them confess that they had been spying for our government. "That was not just a case of native barbarity," one of the worst-treated among them has testified. "They simply couldn't grasp the idea that a foreign correspondent was not doubling as a spy." And in the five years before Pearl Harbor, the offices of the Japanese correspondents in New York and the Pacific cities seemed to the casual observer very much overstaffed.

Possibly the Germans in World War II have made less use of blackmail, and of defective characters as personnel, than in past wars. Or rather perhaps the kind of blackmail has changed. Once they bored into the private lives of rakes, homosexuals, amorous statesmen, and cheating married women and forced them into service by threat of exposure. Such people, having damaged characters, seldom made wholly satisfactory spies. Falsity was inherent in many among them; and unless military information is reasonably accurate, it is worse than useless. The modern method is to use Germans or citizens of conquered nations who adhere to the Nazi doctrine, and hold their relatives in the old country as hostages. The Nazis tried this on William Sebold, the young German-American who performed such brave and intelligent counterespionage in the famous case of the eight saboteurs of 1942. However, the Nazis did not confine this process to Germans only. They forced sailors on the free ships of occupied countries to spy for them by the threat of having their families stood up against a wall. When we rounded up stray seamen of invaded nations in the port of New York, we put them in the detention quarters of Ellis Island, along with dangerous enemy aliens awaiting deportation—and presently it was discovered that the Germans were trying to recruit the newcomers as spies!

Every spy should have some preliminary training. The man or men who procure him may attend to that. But during World War I Colonel Nicolai, able director of German espionage and propaganda, developed the idea of schools where spies could receive systematic instruction from experts. From among the pupils in the first experimental schools emerged Elsbeth Schragmüller, who was to become a legendary figure as the "Fräulein Doktor."

When the war began, she had just received her degree of Doctor of Philosophy at the University of Freiburg and gave promise of a brilliant career in scholarship. She was a slight, blonde, blue-eyed, prepossessing girl, when for no other motive than hot patriotism she volunteered as a clerk at the Office of Censorship in captured Brussels and found so many useful facts that other censors had overlooked as to attract attention in Berlin. German intelligence sent her to a spy school, where she proved brilliant and original; and when the Germans consolidated the work into one "college" at Antwerp, they made her its general director.

Legend has transformed her into a subtle she-devil. In cold truth she was merely a severe and very able schoolmistress. She did not hesitate to procure murder when one of her own spies proved indiscreet or faithless; but in that she was only following the rules of the game as the Germans see it. Hers was, of course, a peculiar school. She held to the sound theory that the less one spy knew about any other spy for his own side, the better. The students worked alone in little rooms and received mostly individual instruction. They entered and left by hidden doors, and separately. When it was necessary for them to attend lectures, they wore masks.

The curriculum included instruction in mapreading and mapmaking, codes and ciphers, invisible writing, concealing notes and documents, detailed study of foreign military and naval equipment and organization, counterespionage in the countries where they were going to work, devices for communication, and a kind of postgraduate course in purely psychological methods, such as escaping attention, shadowing, eluding shadows, and gathering information without showing one's own hand.

Since the affair of the saboteurs, we know that Germany kept up this educational work in World War II. William Sebold, our counterspy, having "volunteered" after a German official had threatened harm to his family in Germany if he refused, attended such an institution at Hamburg. The general curriculum was the same as that in the Fräulein Doktor's establishment, but with modern additions such as microphotography, the use and construction of ultra-short-wave radio apparatus, and economic espionage. Further, there is a school for saboteurs, which graduated the six German agents whom we executed in 1942. German schools have trained Japanese spies, and German teachers have been assigned to Japanese spy schools.

The qualifications for entrance to these schools are personal rather than intellectual. The candidate must speak some foreign language fluently. If he speaks it without a trace of accent, so much the better. However, a slight touch of alien speech is not an insuperable obstacle, especially in espionage against the United States. We are accustomed to loyal citizens with foreign accents; the "dialect" spy can therefore escape notice by blending with this element. If the matriculate has lived long in the country where he is expected to work, so much the better; he will know his way about.

His mind and temperament undergo special scrutiny. Contrary to what one would expect, the ideal spy in the rank and file lacks imagination. What the expert intelligence officer wants is meticulous accuracy in collecting and transmitting details. The higher staff will furnish the invention and creation. Inference and conjecture from the spy himself only blur the picture. The nervous and dramatic temperament is barred; the spy should be fundamentally stolid, quiet rather than voluble, cool and poker-faced in emergency. Provided his loyalty seems certain, his superiors will not look too narrowly into his personal habits—with one exception: alcohol loosens the tongue and brushes away inhibitions; therefore, men who cannot "take it or leave it" are decidedly not wanted. Exception to the exception: some jobs require a man who drinks but who has proved that he knows how to hold his liquor. And, of course, he must have no scars, disfigurements, or other conspicuous physical peculiarities. A popular motion picture showed a spy with a club foot—which was pure Hollywood.

In theory, any corps of spies is organized like an army or navy, with a general staff, a board of strategy, a field commander for every separate front, and so on. But there are several practical differences, the main one rising from the necessity for secrecy not only as regards the enemy, but within the corps itself. A body of spies intimately acquainted with each other would be at the mercy of any member who turned traitor or lost his nerve when arrested; and, to repeat, secret service is dealing constantly with agents who are defective morally. This applies especially to the lower ranks of the profession. In the perfect arrangement, the private in this army would know only the immediate superior who has recruited him, delivers his pay, and gives him orders. Even his "drop"— the place where he deposits his information—might be only a letter box. We speak of a "spy ring"; it would be more accurate to compare it to a chain, whereof each link touches only the links to right and left. However,

this business deals with all human life; and human affairs
are so complex and unpredictable that circumstances are
always modifying the arrangement. Oddly, the expert
Germans seem to depart from it more often than their
enemies—perhaps because Germans in general lack the
inherent self-reliance of the Americans, the British, and
the French and work and fight best when they feel themselves shoulder to shoulder with their comrades. Perhaps,
too, this is why some of their agencies have held to a
"mass-production" doctrine of espionage. They send out
many chains of spies, often including individuals with
whom they are taking a risk. This leads to frequent arrests and damaging exposures. Their chiefs of intelligence admit this, but contend that the great bulk of information they receive by this system outbalances the
disadvantages. The British have always leaned toward
the opposite theory. They have favored quality rather
than quantity and the use of individual methods. British spies are usually men and women of brains, resource
and special inherent qualifications for the job, including character and fidelity; and so far as possible they
play a lone hand. Their personal superiority probably
accounts for the fact that relatively few British spies are
caught by the enemy. The British intelligence service,
especially the diplomatic branch, is often called the best
in the world.

CHAPTER THREE

THE SPY: WHAT HE DOES, AND HOW

IT is relatively easy to classify modern spies according to their character and origins. Classifying their operations and methods is more difficult. Once, the sole object of military espionage was to uncover the secret plans of statesmen and the strategical or tactical intentions of armies. But the range of secret service has grown enormously with the years. World War I was not six months old before all belligerents realized that machines were becoming as important to warfare as men and that the capacity to produce, or some new invention for wholesale killing, might be the key to victory. Hence secret service, spreading out far behind the lines, began looking into the enemy's factories and even into his sources of raw materials. Germany and Britain were trying to starve each other out, the one by submarine warfare against merchant vessels, the other by naval blockade. To know the destination, sailing date, and cargo of every ship on the seven seas was to hold a powerful weapon; hence the ports of the world swarmed with spies and counterspies for one belligerent or the other.

Finally, the spy took on a new task—physical this

time, not mental. If he could destroy munitions or raw materials "on the shelf" as well as merely give information about them, so much the better. The process known as sabotage is as old as warfare. The Indian brave used to sneak into our cavalry camps and stampede or kill horses; Confederate agents destroyed or damaged the arms in Union arsenals during our Civil War. But only in World War I did the practice begin to be recognized as standard. We were perhaps the chief sufferers. In our period of neutrality, agents serving under Papen and Boy-Ed of the Central Powers burned or blew up merchant ships by the dozen, engineered strikes, mislabeled consignments, damaged machinery, caused the great Black Tom and Kingsland explosions. And on our side, agents for the subject peoples of Austria—led by a Russian known to tradition only as "the Devil"—planted time bombs in the factories of Bohemia and Austrian Poland. In the current war, this process has almost reached the dignity of a separate arm of the service. However, we shall treat of sabotage in a later chapter.

There are so many aspects of modern war—military, naval, economic, political, social—that the spymaster who tried to cover them all would face a hopeless task. The spy in our country confines himself to some definite assignment or set of assignments. Usually, his superiors at Berlin or Tokio have already made the choice for him. Take, for example, the intercepted instructions of Commander Sadatomo Okada of the Japanese Navy— he worked in the United States before Pearl Harbor—to his spies. He wanted to know about—

sailings of merchant ships, mobilization of reserve officers and men, the launchings of specific types of cruisers. Any preparation for fleet maneuvers. The methods of training used for army and navy aviation. The training given relative to bad weather conditions over sea and land, the capacity of shipyards for the building of warships. The progress of shipbuilding in navy yards or private construction companies. Information concerning any agreement between Great Britain and the United States concerning the joint use of bases and the training methods utilized in the United States based upon European methods, including air attacks on ships.

These instructions specifically excluded information regarding the situation in our Pacific Islands, where Japan seemed adequately served by other spies, and covered only a fraction of what the general staff of a navy would want to know about an enemy. On many other points, perhaps, the Japanese Navy felt itself well enough informed; these were the special facts in which it was most interested at the time.

Just so, when Commander Itaru Tachibana ran afoul of our F.B.I., agents found in his rooms data classified under headings such as "Placing submarines into service and submarine construction capacity"; "Schedule of United States merchant ships to the Orient"; "Outlook of shipments of planes to Australia and the Netherlands East Indies"; "Altitude of horizontal bombing and number of planes in a formation."

Each spy had his separate task. And each spymaster, like the city editor of a newspaper, probably assigned his white or yellow assistants to one or two definite jobs. One, for example, might be the proprietor of a Japanese resort frequented by sailors. Some of his waiters or jitney dancers would be subagents. They would keep their ears open for data bearing on the sailing dates and cargoes of merchant ships. Thompson, the former navy yeoman convicted in 1938 of espionage for Japan, was typical of this class. He used to put on the old uniform, and as a friendly visitor board warships anchored at San Pedro or Long Beach, California. Once aboard, he maneuvered to get into officers' quarters and steal or copy confidential documents relating largely to gunnery and fleet tactics.

Such operatives are termed fixed-post spies. They stay in one place, usually finding and imparting mere fragments of information. In the long period of locked lines that marked World War I, innumerable spies of this class specialized in troop movements. During our battle of the Meuse-Argonne in 1918, a map of the Western front hung in general headquarters at Chaumont; numbers pinned on it, and changed daily, marked the location of every German division whether in the line or in reserve. This information came from trench raids and aerial reconnaissance; but also from those "train watchers"—station employees, maintenance workers, or simply people living near railroads—whom Major General Dennis E. Nolan, Chief of Intelligence for the A.E.F., considered the most useful spies of all. Often this tedious process had important results. In October, 1917, an Austro-German army broke through the Italian line at Caporetto, killed or captured a whole Italian army, and overran the province of Friuli. It seemed probable that they would either go on to put Italy out of the war or, turning westward, attack France. Through the gap of the

Riviera, the French and British rushed 200,000 men by railroad to the line of the Piave. Even before they arrived, the German and Austrian staffs knew the numbers and units of this reinforcement, and decided to dig in and stay where they were. The knowledge came from train watchers stationed along the Paris-Lyon-Méditerannée railroad who merely reported the number of cars in troop trains that passed through a given point, together with the insignia on the uniforms of their passengers. In the early part of the present war, when our support of the United Nations was limited to lend-lease, spies on fixed post in our great Atlantic ports flashed the sailing dates and cargoes of ships bound for France or Britain. This was done for the benefit of submarine commanders, as in the *Robin Moore* case. In spite of our counterespionage, some of this is still going on.

The fixed-post spy is not always a small operator. The class includes such agents as highly placed society women, employees in government bureaus or in munitions plants, and officers who have wormed their way into general staffs. Sometimes such people by one brilliant or lucky stroke surprise a confidence or capture a document giving information that intelligence officers and squads of spies have been trying for months to patch together. Early in 1918 a Czech officer at Austrian headquarters, a proud traitor to his emperor but loyal to his race, sent across the lines to the Italian General Diaz the detailed plans for a proposed Austrian summer campaign. Going further back, Mrs. Rose O'Neale Greenhow, Confederate spy at Washington, on July 16, 1861, got through to General Beauregard the message: "Orders issued for McDowell to move on Manassas tonight." On those nine words Allan Pinkerton, Lincoln's chief of secret service, placed the responsibility for the disastrous Union defeat at Bull Run.

Thus the "station" of a fixed spy may be as low as a ginmill near a navy yard, or as high as the anteroom of a monarch. Once, we turned up a suspect in the black chamber (code and cipher room) of the War Department. After the last war, the British discovered that the Germans had had a spy in the office of mail censorship. His efficiency was his undoing. He made himself so useful that the British kicked him upstairs to a position of higher responsibility in which he had no opportunity to find out anything important. In this country, a German spy owned and ran a radio shop where he not only picked up military information but supplied communications for an entire ring. Still another was a stamp dealer, who sought and found contact with collectors eminent in the government.

There are simple jobs in espionage, such as establishing sailing dates of ships or getting at one particular document; there are complex ones, such as finding the complete battle tactics of an army or navy. The spy can seldom do such a job while nailed to one locality. Thus we have the traveling spy who may be in New York one week and in Detroit the next. Usually he has a plausible excuse for his wanderings—salesman for an established firm, or technical investigator for some engineering company. Kurt Ludwig and his secretary Miss Lucy Boehmler, mentioned before, were traveling spies. Evidently, Ludwig was assigned to two main "lines of investigation": aircraft construction and the extent and pattern of our military preparation. The first part of his assignment he farmed out, temporarily at least, to the able and dangerous Helen Pauline Mayer. With her husband, she cultivated the acquaintance of workers in plants making aircraft and pumped them so cleverly that only her arrest by the F.B.I. prevented her from getting very damaging information to Germany.

Ludwig and Lucy Boehmler undertook the second part of the assignment. By train and car, they traveled from New York through the East and Middle West, he talking to soldiers on trains or uniformed hitchhikers on the roads, she picking up acquaintances in the resorts that surround a military post, and both going through camps and plants or watching maneuvers as visitors or spectators. His work had one essentially weak point: he failed to find any plausible business connection. A lone man traveling near army camps accompanied by a presentable young girl and having no apparent reason for his travels was a suspected person.

These roving spies serve another purpose. Often they stumble upon promising lines of investigation which their superiors have not envisioned, or startling facts which no one could have foreseen—in which case the well-trained spy tips off the fact to his superiors, exactly as a good newspaper reporter will do when in working on one story he stumbles onto another. In 1918, a valuable agent working on the Netherlands border for our army concerned himself mainly with keeping track of poison gases. But through one of his informants he got the first hint of those long-range Big Berthas that bombarded Paris that summer. Later, he found and reported the location of one of them, enabling the French to bomb it from the air.

How do spies like Ludwig, Lucy Boehmler and Helen Mayer wring information out of their victims? Although intelligence departments have been trying for seventy-five years to transform espionage into a science, pumping an unsuspecting prospect remains a personal art, like salesmanship. And it is impossible to reduce an art to a set of formulas. The Fräulein Doktor, however, drew up a few simple and wise rules for the spies whom she educated at Antwerp. The instructors of the spy schools at Hamburg and Berlin are drilling these rules into pupils today; so doubtless are the spyteachers in the United Nations. She wrote:

When gathering information do not seem to be curious or anxious to obtain it.

Train the face to be absolutely impassive. Obtain important intelligence by inventing information in the course of the conversation, and expounding it with an air of mystery. [Here she might have added that a touch of skepticism or a little friendly argument often helps.]

Do not speak of confidential subjects in trains, on streetcar platforms, or in cabs.

Conceal the knowledge of a given language so far as possible, in order to overhear the conversation of others.

Appointments with persons from whom information is expected should be made in some place as far as possible from their place of residence, and from the agent's field of operation. It is even advisable to have them travel several hours by train, especially at night, for when men are tired they are more expansive and less cautious than otherwise.

Be satisfied with ascertaining half a dozen facts rather than a hundred opinions. The latter, if expressed by fools, are worth nothing and if expressed by persons of intelligence may not be sincere; the former, although they may not seem important at the time, may lead to appreciable results when once they have been compared with others.

Of course, the spy's information is of no use unless he gets it to headquarters, where the armies or navies can transform thought into action. Furthermore, in many crises of war or preparation for war it is just as useless if it comes too late. When in 1918 the Germans were preparing the Spring drive to break the Western front of the Allies, by one of the cleverest operations in the history of espionage and counterespionage they deceived French and British intelligence into believing that their extensive preparations were aimed at the French on the Champagne sector. Instead, the Germans attacked the British along the Somme, where the blow came as a complete surprise. While the Western trench line still rumbled along in its dreary rhythm and the communiqués reported "all quiet," a reliable French spy had sent positive proof of their real intentions; but the message did not arrive until a week after the Germans went over the top.

Ever since warfare began to grow complex and scientific, prompt and reliable communication has been the chief problem of espionage. In the archaic period when two relatively small and compact armies marched on foot and after a little maneuvering came to grips for a battle lasting a day or two, the typical spy simply sneaked into the enemy lines in disguise, came back and reported to the general or his aide. But even then, there were spies on fixed post or otherwise so situated that they must put their information on paper. And today, the operations of any army and navy may spread as wide as the world; in 1942, we Americans had troops and warships on all the six continents and seven seas. No naked voice can carry so far as that. Also, experience has taught intelligence officers that oral communications may be dangerously inaccurate. The spy works under a subconscious strain that plays strange tricks with memory, and he deals in modern times with figures and technical details. An error of one hundredth of an inch in describing a machine part may render his information worse than useless. When it comes to maps, diagrams, or blueprints of a military position, a bomb sight or a new tank, very few people have sufficient visual memory to carry the perfect image in their minds. "Paper work" is necessary, and has been so since man invented writing.

Very early in the game mathematicians invented codes and ciphers for secret communication. The Romans used them; Friar Roger Bacon disguised with them the scientific discoveries which his age would have regarded as heretical; Benjamin Franklin played with them as a diversion. Perhaps not all readers understand the distinction between codes and ciphers. When, as constantly happens in private correspondence—and especially in love

letters—the writer substitutes an arbitrary word for another word, phrase, or sentence, that constitutes a code.
We use codes constantly in commercial telegrams, partly
by way of economy, partly to conceal business secrets.
For example, in the old maritime code the word "wob-
ble" signified "shall I notify owners?" In the same way,
when the British Army fought the battle of Messines
Ridge, Field Marshal Sir Douglas Haig figured in their
code as "Handsome Willie."

A cipher or cryptogram, on the other hand, consists in
juggling with letters or whole words by some mathematical process. The simplest form appears on the puzzle page of the newspapers, where the composer baffles
us by consistently substituting one letter of the alphabet
for another; for example, *h* for *a, i* for *n, g* for *d,* changes
and to *hig.* The processes, going on from there, infringe
on higher mathematics; to describe them in detail would
require a whole treatise. The spy first puts his message
into code and then into cipher. When it emerges, it is an
arbitrary, meaningless string of numbers or of numbers
and letters, usually arranged in groups. The German
spies rounded up in the United States before Pearl Harbor had a "book key" for their ciphers—one of them a
no less American work than the first edition of Rachel
Field's *All This and Heaven Too.* It began very simply.
First the constructor wrote his message. Then from this
book he picked the first word he wanted and set down
three numbers—say 56, 7, 5—representing the page, line,
and word in that line. Then he juggled with the higher
arithmetic. Finally, the message was always dated; and

the mathematical process differed for each day of the week. "Crack" a message dated on a Tuesday, and the counterspy had to begin all over again to find the formula for one dated on a Friday.

The ciphers used in World War I now seem to the expert decipherer as simple as newspaper puzzles. For their increased complexity and difficulty of solution in this war, the humble American bootlegger stands partly responsible. The rumrunners of our prohibition era communicated with their confederates ashore by radio and cipher codes; the coast guard intercepted the messages and set experts to deciphering them; the bootleggers countered by employing high mathematicians to invent more complicated ciphers on new principles; the coast guard cross-countered by cracking them also, thereby learning more than even the bootlegger knew about both the construction and deciphering of codes and ciphers. The knowledge is doing good service for us in this war. Meantime, "machine ciphers" have arrived. The name explains them; they are to the old process as is the adding machine to the bookkeeper's pad and pencil. The common type of machine has several wheels, one for plain text, the others for various ciphers, according to how the wheels are set. The machines of all correspondents are set in the same way; that is the real key to a machine cipher. Some are so small that they may be strapped onto the operator's knee. The obvious advantages are speed and accuracy; but their product is also exceedingly hard to crack.

The small spies will be incapable of such mental processes. They pass on their findings orally to the next spy in the chain. If he be really expert in his business, he has learned his code by heart, even though one code cracked by our F.B.I. experts consisted of more than seven hundred words with corresponding phrases. Equally well does he know the formula for his cipher. If his group is sending messages by radio, the enemy has intercepted some of them and experts are at work finding the formulas. It will be only a question of time before they succeed. Hence both codes and ciphers must be changed from time to time. William Sebold, our invaluable secret agent against the Duquesne group of spies and the eight saboteurs, brought overseas a new code in the form of a microphotograph no bigger than a special delivery stamp, which he hid in the back of his watch.

The next link in the chain of espionage is the "drop" where the sender sees the last of his message—unless a court-martial introduces it into evidence when he stands trial for his life! He may simply hand it over to the next link in the chain, the man who procured him in the first place; there it goes to a collector, operating under a good camouflage, or to some secret radio station for transmission by ultra-short-wave radio; he may send it by air mail to some address in a neutral country like Portugal or the Argentine; he may use a kind of clearinghouse. Such a one, in the days when Duquesne and Ludwig were active, was a small bookstore in Yorkville, the German district of New York. Parenthetically, after the F.B.I. found the trail, it shadowed known German agents who from time to time visited the shop, made a purchase, and in the course of the transaction slipped an envelope to the clerk. The establishment, using a rubber stamp, always printed its name and address on the flyleaves of its stock. Searching the room of a suspect, the F.B.I. men found this mark on an obscure blood-and-thunder novel. Was this perhaps the key to their book cipher? Our experts went to work on this theory—and cracked the cipher.

A spy letter that travels by an international route must not trust to code and cipher alone. It may come to the attention of a censor; and a meaningless jumble of figures and letters would send it at once to the deciphering bureau. Most of them are written in invisible ink. That, like cipher, is a very old device. Certain organic or inorganic chemical substances—lemon juice and dissolved aspirin, for example—laid carefully on hard-finished paper dry out perfectly white; but appropriate chemical reagents will lend color to them. Chemists are constantly inventing new invisible inks. Kurt Ludwig, for example, had in his possession a bottle of tablets of a hitherto unknown formula. The spy writes an apparently honest letter, on the letterhead of an existent and innocent firm or of a dummy organization, and with a ball-pointed pen (so as not to scratch the paper) adds the message in invisible ink between the lines or on the back. No censorship can treat with a dozen reagents all the mail passing by ship or airplane to such neutral countries as Spain and Portugal. Mostly the censors at such points as the British control in Bermuda so treat only those letters that have some suspicious feature such as the suggestion of a German idiom or German penmanship or that bear the signatures or addresses of persons on the suspect lists.

Soldiers say that no device of warfare no matter how antique ever quite passes out of use. Men first fought with clubs and knives; and our marines in the jungles of the East Indies are using these primitive weapons today. Before we had the telegraph, radio, railroads, or organized mails, the spymaster used couriers for distant communications, and they are important even yet. Generally, although not universally, they do no spying of their own but only carry the data to headquarters and the orders back to working agents. Sometimes they are indispensable, as in the case of a change in cipher or code. They are especially active during the period when the war cloud is gathering and ships still ply between ports of the prospective belligerents. In 1939 and 1940, the German liners between New York and Hamburg not only carried Nazi couriers among the passengers but there was a regular service staffed by members of the crews.

Johanna Hofmann, hairdresser on the liner *Europa,* served in the late 1930's as courier for the Rumrich group of spies who were industriously gathering data on our plans to defend our coast. Probably the F.B.I., then just beginning its work of counterespionage, touched only the edge of this industry. Couriers were traveling on all German liners and on most neutral ships. In World War I, the Dutch lines were favorite accommodations for German couriers. On the steamer *Rotterdam,* British and Czech counterespionage in 1916 trapped F. J. F.

Archibald, American courier for the Austrians, who had deposited in the supposed security of the ship's safe a huge package of written information, but somehow rid himself of a hollow cane containing plans and diagrams of military works. Before June, 1941, Germany and Russia were parties to a nonaggression pact; and the communist element in neutral countries was momentarily helping the Germans all they could. We know now that communists on ships of many flags were at that time active as couriers. Picking up the messages at New York, they would hand them over to German or Japanese spies in neutral ports. Although the war has since spread so widely that there are few neutrals, couriers are still plying between Portugal or Spain and London. In 1942, the British hanged Duncan Scott-Ford as a traitor. A seaman on that run, he had been corrupted by a German agent in Lisbon. He had not only carried messages, but kept tabs on the sailing dates of merchant ships for the benefit of submarines.

Many of the great spy tales, true and fictional, deal with the adventures of couriers—Major Rowan carrying the "message to Garcia"; Villa Voska, sixteen-year-old American girl traveling from Prague across Germany and Holland to Kitchener in London with Thomas Masaryk's data on the Austrian Army wrapped around the steels of her old-fashioned corset; the classic American play *Secret Service*. The tricks for concealing messages on their persons were innumerable, as were the devices for disposing of them when trapped. By the time of World War I, there appeared a Japanese rice paper thinner than the finest natural membrane. A genius in miniature craftsmanship who worked for the Slavic rebels against Austria could write a comparatively long message on a small sheet of this paper and enclose it in the shell of a wooden match stem. Other places of concealment about the person were hollow soles of shoes, the quills in the feathers of a woman's hat, a cigarette, the works of a watch, a hole under the filling of a tooth, the interior of an overcoat button or a bone hairpin, tablets and capsules in medicine bottles, false bottoms of bags and other luggage—but the list would make a catalogue. Sometimes the message, especially if it be an official order going back from headquarters to the actual spies, is written on the skin of the courier's back in invisible ink; and probably many a humble courier, believing himself trapped, has disposed of the damning evidence by taking an unaccustomed bath.

Destroying a message in case of capture has always been a problem. The old, standard method was to swallow it; and when that was done some of the tough border guards of World War I made cathartics and emetics a part of their third degree when they detained a suspect. The Germans have developed a paper that dissolves when swallowed. One Allied courier put his papers into the bowl of his pipe; when real danger loomed, he filled up and took a smoke. Now, probably, microphotography has generally supplanted rice paper. If a whole code of many hundreds of words and phrases can be recorded on the area of a postage stamp, as we stated before, a simple signed order from headquarters might fill an area no larger than the paring of a nail. The "radio-photo" process, by means of which a New York news-paper reproduces today a photograph taken yesterday in Russia, is susceptible to use by secret service. A classic example in old days was a harmless drawing of a butter-fly carried among the papers of an alleged entomologist.

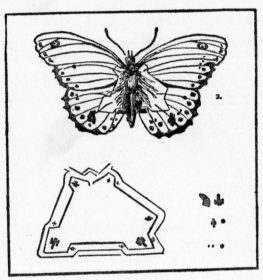

The Butterfly Trick

Eliminate certain lines by certain rules, and it became the map of a fortress. Today such a drawing could be flashed around the world. And there are new tricks of concealment about which we can say nothing until after the war.

Standard couriers for such messages in old times were

carrier pigeons; their use goes back to remote antiquity. Medieval records mention the use of sparrows for the same purpose, but tantalizingly add no details as to their breed or training. Armies of the past, notably the Germans in the Franco-Prussian War, trained falcons or hawks to intercept homing pigeons and bring them down with the messages still fastened at their necks. Pigeons remain an instrument of espionage, else the Nazis would not be shooting inhabitants of Czechoslovakia and the Balkans on the charge of possessing them illegally.

To come up to the more recent present, wireless telegraphy and telephony have almost transformed the field of communications. In World War I, Marconi's invention had got no further than the stage of transmission of the Morse telegraphic code. Sending long range required an enormous apparatus; the great wireless installation of the Germans at Nauen and the one at Mexico City were the only stations capable of reaching across the Atlantic. Employed mainly for propaganda, the Nauen wireless station sent, also, messages in a five-group "number" cipher which, when our experts cracked it, turned out to be directions to spies and propagandists. The relatively small portable apparatus used as liaison between military units at the front had a range of only thirty miles or so. Army divisions and also spies operating near the trench line used this method of communication. Wireless interception was advanced enough so that counter-espionage could pick up the dispatches. Therefore it was necessary to send by code and cipher. Both sides changed the code or the key every five or six weeks. A historic story of the American Expeditionary Force is worth repeating here. We had cracked a German cipher-code. The enemy suspected this and changed to a new one. Our listeners picked up a message in the new code from a German sender. It was Greek to them. Then back from the German receiving station came this stupid reply: "Do not understand you. Repeat in old code." With equal stupidity, the sender obeyed. With the words in the old code as a key, we had cracked the new one in less than twenty-four hours.

There are other devices, the only limit being the bounds of human ingenuity. In World War I, a harmless technical journal published in Britain had on its masthead a picture of a flock of bees surrounding a hive. Copies had been going to Switzerland for two years before the British censors discovered that the number and arrangement of the bees varied from week to week, and then that on the mailed copy some of them were not printed but added to the picture with India ink. This constituted the code of an inventive spy. The stamp dealer, referred to previously, sent and received consignments of collector's items between the United States and a neutral country. The notches on the margins were marked in a peculiar way—again a cipher. In World War I, the A.E.F. used a unique device both for guarding and transmitting secret matter. The American Indian has a curious talent for inventing languages. On this continent are thousands of tongues bearing no relation to one another—and in many instances unknown to any white man. Two Indians of the same tribe talking

SCIENTIFIC METHODS. A TECHNICIAN OF THE F.B.I. ANALYZING STAINS ON AN ENVELOPE.

Brown Brothers

THE END OF THE MERCENARY SPY. FOUR FRENCH CITIZENS, ONE (LEFT) A WOMAN, SHOT IN THE WOOD OF VINCENNES FOR ESPIONAGE ON BEHALF OF THE GERMANS.

over a telephone or radio constitute the undecipherable code. And so on.

Now, we have the short-wave and ultra-short-wave radio which transmit not only dots and dashes but the human voice. "You can carry a short-wave sender in a suit case; you can set it up in a cellar," someone has remarked. That is an exaggeration but not a very great one. With a comparatively small apparatus, one can talk across oceans. Wireless interception, however, has kept pace with wireless transmission. The very ether above us is at war. We can even approximately locate the situation of a transmitting station by the "beam" process. The spies know that, and they constantly change their base of operations. The art of interception is not yet a perfect one. Messages slip through uncaught. But enough are caught to make code and cipher important as never before. One cannot risk plain language. The decipherers, working with calculating machines and mathematical formulas supplemented by human experience and shrewdness, are at it twenty-four hours a day. Part of the game consists in concealing from the enemy the fact that you have solved the problem of his code and cipher key, so that he will continue to use it. And the enemy may counter by sending a fake test message and observing whether or not your military forces act on the information.

Finally, how do armies, navies, and chancellors get spies into enemy territory? We have answered part of that question. The Axis Powers, which planned, expected, and wanted war, planted them at their posts in advance. Thousands of German agents disguised as tourists, students, and businessmen infested France, Poland, Norway, and the Low Countries. Some of them were neutrals serving mostly for money; some, natives converted to the fascist doctrine. When the blitzkrieg came, these people not only sent information but gave such active service as guiding invaders, blowing up bridges, transmitting false orders by telephone or telegraph, and spreading dire rumors. And, per contra, even though the democracies had been working on the theory that you can appease hell-fire, their own intelligence departments had spies established in Germany, Italy, and Japan.

As regards us, our European enemy believed that in the German-American population, as inspired by the Bund and kindred organizations, they had an inexhaustible reservoir of secret agents for both propaganda and espionage. That was not the first nor yet the last time that Germany made a gross blunder in reading human psychology. Germany sowed the wind and reaped the whirlwind. As she settled down onto her conquered lands, she installed her own peculiar system of robbery, looting, murder, and starvation. With the Gestapo and the army watching for every sign of organized resistance, patriotism had only one outlet: secret service on behalf of the nations that could still resist openly. There followed a unique episode in history: an underground war beyond all precedent for range, for numbers involved, or for bitterness. In the little democracies of western Europe, the enlisted personnel of these patriot armies almost outnumber the uniformed armies who so briefly resisted the invader. And considering the thousands shot as spies, saboteurs, and "communists," the tens of thousands who have perished in concentration camps, so do the dead in action.

In western Europe these secret agencies, springing up spontaneously in all the occupied countries, at first carried on sabotage, espionage, and secret propaganda without expert direction or clear objectives. Then the governments-in-exile, the British intelligence departments, the Free French, and some of the best minds and spirits in the enslaved territory organized these valiant patriots, gave their work direction and meaning. The United States was no sooner in the war than we began to help— and on no mean scale. Thanks partly to American money, the number of surreptitious newspapers in occupied territory had by 1943 grown to 1,500. The Dutch revived the Beggars, that oath-bound secret society which under William of Orange harried Spain out of the Netherlands; the Norwegians have created a web of secret agents that spreads into every hamlet of the plucky little kingdom; the Czechs, who under Austrian rule kept their national faith for three hundred years, have proved masters of sabotage; in the depressed hell which is wartime Poland the delegates of two hundred underground agencies astoundingly held a convention—also underground—during the autumn of 1942; and they all work not in hit-and-miss fashion but according to a system, directed largely from London but in increasing collaboration with one another.

Dangerous all this; a higher test of courage and fortitude than ordeal by battle. When these countries regain their liberties, no honor their governments pay can give adequate reward to the devotion of these plain European people who have walked through the fire and kept the faith. By the power of the spirit they have overcome the power of the flesh. Shootings in Norway and Poland and the Netherlands, hangings in western Russia, mass executions of young men in Serbia, Lidice in Czechoslovakia, constant murder of hostages—these served the German cause not at all. Every drop of blood the Gestapo spilled was martyr-seed from which sprang ten more spies against them.

As for the Russians and the Russian-occupied part of Poland, the machinery was ready when the Germans overran them. The Russians have a special talent for underground action, and in preparing for the expected attack they envisaged the probability that their armies might be driven far eastward before they could stand and counterattack. At every withdrawal, they left behind not only those guerillas and snipers of whom we read so much in the newspapers, but organized spies and saboteurs in great numbers; these forces were a main reason for the declining fortunes of Germany's Army of the East during 1942. Not only that: the Third International, the foreign branch of the Communist party, had organized for world revolution in all countries. Already half underground when the war began, after the invasion of Russia they burrowed deeper and became a secret service, sometimes performing useless acts of violence, more often doing work of real value to the United Nations. In Yugoslavia, the partisans of this faction have passed on to open warfare against the Germans and Italians. By 1943 this communist underground movement was growing in all eastern and middle Europe. The Third International is becoming a lone wolf. Stalin and his faction have been moving from internationalism toward nationalism; and there are signs that these turbulent revolutionaries are breaking away from his guidance. Their backfires against the Nazis may cause embarrassing complications, like a Red war at the time when the German armies begin to crack under pressure. After one of his victories, Frederick the Great boasted: "Marshal de Soubise was followed by a hundred cooks; I was preceded by a hundred spies." The United Nations will invade continental Europe preceded by ten million spies; and unlike Frederick's they will not be paid help. This is their fight.

However, it is still necessary to send spies to and from hostile European territory, even if they are only couriers bringing orders or new code and cipher-keys—and especially for the Germans who are barred from the high seas. "Running the borders" is one method. No army can guard any frontier perfectly. During World War I, Switzerland was the spy center of Europe; just as is Portugal nowadays. And with comparatively little trouble, Allied spies were always slipping over into Germany, Austrian and German spies into France. Today, in spite of the Gestapo, refugees from Holland, Belgium, Norway, and France are constantly arriving in London or Lisbon. If they find a way out, there must be a way in.

Often, during World War I, spies with linguistic talents traveled in enemy territory carrying the passports of neutral countries—forged, bought, or virtually stolen. Forgery and doctoring of passports became a high art. In Madrid, another spy center, the standard price of a genuine American passport before April, 1917, was two hundred dollars. Captain Karl Hans Lody, the first German spy shot by the British, was carrying the papers of an American whose passport the German authorities at Hamburg had conveniently "lost." The Czechoslovak and south Slav rebels in the United States found means to steal blank passports from the Austrian consulate at New York for couriers into Austrian territory. One of the couriers was Charles Steiger, naturalized American citizen, carrying, of course, American credentials; he traveled in the guise of a salesman. Months after he left, the newspapers reported that Charles Steiger, an Austrian spy holding an American passport, had been caught in France with a message in invisible ink written on his back, and shot. Six months after that, Steiger bobbed up in New York, alive but not well. Never suspecting his mission in Europe, the Austrians, who needed an American passport badly at the moment, had arrested him on some flimsy charge, forged the required visas on his impounded passport, juggled a little with the photograph and the signature, and handed it to the ill-fated spy. Such maneuvers are still going on. Osten, slated for German spymaster in the United States during the current war, carried a Spanish passport—whether a forgery or a favor from Franco, only the German Government and the F.B.I. know.

The spyhunters must watch refugees closely. The Germans often slip agents into those pathetic caravans. Lilly Stein, convicted of espionage in 1941, took advantage of looks inherited from a remote Jewish ancestor to enter the United States as a fugitive from anti-Semitic persecution. She damned Hitler publicly and worked for him privately. A graduate of a German spy school, she seems to be one of those people whose promise excel their performance. Her maneuvers were somewhat transparent: her intercepted correspondence with Germany consisted mostly of appeals for funds and of clippings from our newspapers.

Much of the above applies to the period when war is brewing. After the guns begin to roar, the chief modern spy carrier is the airplane. It began its work in the last half of World War I. Just at dawn, a light, two-seater plane would soar above a level field in enemy territory and drop by parachute a man with a crate of carrier pigeons. Concealing his live stock in the bushes, he would go forth by day disguised as a peasant and at night send his information in a quill hung about a feathered neck. He had a rendezvous with his aviator on the same field a week or ten days afterward, when the pigeons would have been used up. There is a story of one of the pioneer "channel fliers," a hero in France, in aviator's uniform during World War I. As the war went on, other fliers like Gunemer and Fonck became aces and popular idols; he remained obscure. Rumor said that he was *embusqué* —that by influence he had secured some soft post, such as patrolling the air over an interior town. His reputation fell so low that when he appeared on the boulevards

wearing a string of decorations, the gossips merely remarked that his pull must be strong indeed. Only after
the Armistice did the French learn that he was a pioneer
in this business of dropping spies behind the lines—an
especially perilous job, since the Germans had at first
ordained that any aviator caught at it should die, along
with his spy. With the improvement and multiplication
of airplanes and parachutes, the process has now become
standard on all fronts.

In that war, the Germans occasionally landed spies by
submarine. The records of the American Expeditionary
Force include one proved instance—spies at Brest, our
great landing port, who watched the arrivals of troops
and sent their messages by flashlight and in telegraph
code to the lurking U-boat offshore. This process also
has become standard. The Germans used it against us
in the expedition of the eight saboteurs. And it is probable that the United Nations are using it against occupied France, Belgium, Holland, and Norway. A broken
seacoast is almost as hard to guard perfectly as a land-
frontier. Even the vigilance of the coast guard and the
efficiency of the F.B.I. cannot wholly insure us against
better managed and luckier landings than those of the
saboteurs who in 1942 went to prison for long terms or
to the electric chair.

Finally, a word about the boss spies and the co-ordination of information from enemy countries and armies.
While some spies are lone wolves, they are usually arranged in those groups known as rings or chains. Sometimes, by way of checking for accuracy, two groups,

wholly unknown to each other, work on the same job—
as in the German search for samples or blueprints of our
Norden bomb sight. Their field commander must be a
man of parts. Not only does he live, like all the rest, with
a dagger at his own back, but he has the special responsibility for guarding the lives and concealing the operations of his subordinates. Counterspies in enemy country
and enemy spies in neutral territory may raid or rum-
mage his offices at any time. Ever since the German, Japanese, and Russians threw overboard the canons of diplomatic etiquette, the diplomatic bag has been the surest
means of communication. It is not perfect, however.
Even in World War I, a Slavic spy serving the German
embassy at Washington as courier in charge of diplomatic pouches managed to abstract and photograph important documents. By the same token, the consulates in
neutral countries, having diplomatic immunity from
search and the privilege of gathering legitimate commercial information, are theoretically the best caches for secret information. In practice, however, the enemy is always worming spies or paid informers into embassies,
legations, and consulates or even cracking their safes.
Also, communication through diplomatic channels other
than coded radio or cable is slow. A German pouch from
the Argentine must travel from Buenos Aires to Lisbon
by steamer, and at Lisbon it has to be re-sorted before it
goes to Berlin by train or plane. And many important
items, like the news that a convoy has sailed, become
stale and useless within a week or two.

Thus nowadays the spymaster who knows his business

cares for his own records but sees that they are so few, so scrambled, and so disguised that anyone who gets a look at them would have a hard time making them mean anything. He keeps no written roster of his staff. All of them are working under assumed names, and, for added precaution, signing their communications with conventional names or symbols. (Marguerite Harrison was "Q"; a very valuable agent we had in Berlin during 1918 was "H-1"; Lonkowski was "S.E.X.") Real names, assumed names, trade names, addresses and telephone numbers he catalogues in his head. And if he or one of the close assistants who knows his identity has a card-index memory for other names, figures, and details, so much the better; he can digest or memorize the written reports of distant spies and then destroy them. A piece of paper with a few scratches on it may be as dangerous as a booby trap.

Little of the information the spymaster receives and transmits goes to headquarters in its pristine form. The general director, with expert assistants corresponding roughly to the editor and copyreaders of a newspaper, first assembles the information and then assays its importance and reliability. This item is trivial or stale; he "kills" it. This other is worth transmitting. But it comes from a single spy, and he not a very intelligent one. It needs confirmation by one or two better men, perhaps by hints extracted from newspapers and technical journals. This information is not immediately important; it can await further investigation. Three or four small items so fit into each other as to make probable one large fact. Worth taking a chance on that! So, having assembled his budget of news and compressed it to the minimum verbiage consistent with clarity, he translates it into code and cipher and sends it on to his channel of communication.

Intelligence headquarters in Berlin, Tokio, London, or Washington has much the same task; only it is larger and more complex. We have compared the work of high intelligence officers to the solving of a jigsaw puzzle. However, the comparison does not walk on all four feet, because a mechanical puzzle excludes the human element. "Only 20 to 50 per cent of information from spies is both honest and fully accurate," says one authority. The high intelligence office must look out for a hundred slippery possibilities. Is this a fake, forged message, sent by the enemy to deceive him or by a dishonest spy to swindle him? Is this small spy who sends big information a reliable man? Has this head of a spy ring let opinion, prejudice, or conjecture creep into his reports? Two pieces of information seem to contradict each other. Which, if either, is right? Often when he transmits the report of an enemy plan or movement he is not himself absolutely certain; he has acted only on the law of probabilities.

He is dealing with some very faulty human material. Yet even when a whole ring proves inefficient and inaccurate, if he cannot replace them by better spies he keeps them on the job. There is always a chance that even the spy who usually sends chaff and trash may stumble onto something big and come through with a nugget of pure gold.

CHAPTER FOUR

THE SPY IN AMERICA TODAY: ESPIONAGE

Now we come to enemy espionage as it affects the United States, and especially the home front, in the greatest of our wars. First, let us see how it is organized.

During World War I, Colonel Walther Nicolai served as chief of German military espionage and of propaganda. Able and farseeing though he was, he never had a free hand; his ideas were too advanced for the conservative soldiers of the Great General Staff. After the Armistice, he expressed himself in two books which attracted little attention at the time, but which forecast the total espionage that the Nazis were to perfect a decade later. He did not spare his criticism of those who had hampered him. Papen, Boy-Ed and their agents, he said, had boggled the task of organizing espionage, sabotage, propaganda, and subversive activities in the United States. They had been found out; and as the Fräulein Doktor, Germany's great spymistress, remarked tersely "the good spy is the one who isn't caught." By letting optimism get the better of them they had misinformed the German Government on the state of public opinion in the United States and on our potential power to make

76

war. "The entry of the United States was the cause of our defeat. From now on, the British Empire and the United States must be the special targets of German espionage and propaganda. . . . The immigration and race problems in North America directly provoke us to test the high art of espionage on them. . . . Far greater than in the past and the present will the secret power of this service be in the future," he wrote in 1924.

At this time, the German Republic had pledged itself in the Treaty of Versailles to renounce military and political espionage in time of peace. But to the old Junker officers of the German Army and Navy, the treaty was only a scrap of paper and the surrender of 1918 only a setback in Germany's progress toward a place in the sun. Under the republican regime, Nicolai and his associates planned that system of interlocked espionage, sabotage, propaganda, and procured treason which we call the fifth column. Then, just as the Nazis began their final preparations for "the day," stronger, younger, and more ruthless hands wrested from him the scepter of command.

Admiral Wilhelm Canaris, the most eminent spymaster of this era, is to Hitler what Stieber was to Bismarck. Like his great predecessor, he has a talent for advancing himself by personal intrigue. He is so daring that he launched the U-boat saboteurs against our own coasts, so ruthless that he procures murder as an instrument of public policy, yet so devious that to get next door he would walk round the block. The manners of Stieber were cheap and brusque except in the presence of superiors, when he became obsequious. Canaris, by contrast, has one of those finished European personalities infused with charm. From Greek ancestors—one of them a pirate —he got his name, his well-shaped and well-set head, his dark eyes, his engaging manners. He has a mania for secrecy about everything, including especially his own affairs. But it is known that he lives in a Berlin suburb with his attractive wife and adolescent son, that for diversion he gardens, rides, reads detective stories, that he seldom appears in public, and that he is rude only to journalists who try to drag him into the limelight. "You write too much!" he barked at one of them. And his enemies among the Germans call him *Der Schnueffler*— "the snooper."

As a subofficer in the German Navy during World War I, he fought in the losing battle of the Falkland Islands and was interned in the Argentine. Disguised as a stoker, he escaped to Spain. The Germans appointed him naval attaché at Madrid, which, before he had finished, meant chief of espionage for the whole Iberian Peninsula and some of the A.E.F.'s rear areas in France. It was he, probably, who sent from Madrid that premeditatedly careless message by means of which the French trapped and shot Mata Hari, who was becoming an embarrassment to the Germans.

To Canaris as to Hitler the surrender of 1918 came as an unforgivable insult; and like Hitler he devoted his life to avenging it. First we find him an accomplice of those big industrialists who were trying to break down the Weimar Republic. The socialists accused him of plot-

ting the assassination of Liebknecht and Rosa Luxem-
burg; and there is evidence to support the charge. Next
he directed the Marine Brigade, a secret group of reac-
tionary officers trying to rebuild the army and navy in
defiance of the Versailles Treaty. Two of them were
jailed for stealing money from government funds to
finance their cause, and twelve others for plotting against
the republic. But not Canaris. He wormed his way in so
successfully that he became director of naval transport in
the republican Ministry of Marine! He made the post a
pious fraud—a screen for the naval espionage that Germany had foresworn in the Versailles Treaty. Captain
Lohmann, one of his stooges, controlled secret government funds. He and Canaris tapped the till for $6,500,-
000 which they used to prepare the way for a full-time
navy and to produce an antidemocratic motion picture
stabbing the republic in the back. This brought open
scandal; but owing again to the Canaris influence with
the great industrialists, they merely lost their jobs.

Now Hitler enters the story. When in 1929 the big
industrialists decided to back the little demagogue from
Munich, Canaris came out of retirement and opened a
"private detective agency" which was only a screen for
political plots. In this capacity he helped to boost General von Schleicher into the chancellorship of the republic. The general was only a blocking back for Hitler.
When Hitler came to power, Nazi gunmen purged
Schleicher and his wife, and the industrialists found that
in the Austrian housepainter they had made a master
out of their servant. But Canaris, once the tool of the

industrialists, had played his cards so well, had shown such capacity for organization and intrigue, such ruthlessness and yet such devotion to the ideal of an all-dominant Germany, as to win the Führer's special favor. Nicolai was shoved aside to the position of a mere counsellor while Canaris became vice-admiral, full admiral, coordinator of all intelligence, and finally member of the *Unabhaengige Reichsbehörde,* the little inner circle who know Hitler's real plans. Those honors Hitler announced publicly, to the disgust of Canaris who shrinks from publicity as did Jeeter Lester from water. Indeed, he blamed it for a setback of his own fortunes. He had gone to Bulgaria as advance man for those German "tourists" who prepare for conquest. British and Russian counterspies, warned of his importance by Hitler's announcement, put shadows on him, found that his next stop was Syria and got there ahead of him. The Russians stayed ahead. They had a spyhunter in every house, a purge every day, a bullet in the head for every Quisling. And the carefully mustered Ukrainian fifth column marched only before firing squads. Nevertheless, at the beginning of 1943 Canaris was—with certain small reservations—the subdictator of all German military espionage.

Taking his agencies in order, naturally his pet is naval intelligence. In the early 1920's, his original group of foreign and domestic spies, camouflaged as members of a yacht club, were not only snooping around the British, French, Italian, and American navies but were laying the foundation of espionage in foreign ports in anticipation of another U-boat campaign. When Hitler came to

MAIL CENSORS TREATING LETTERS TO BRING OUT INVISIBLE WRITING.

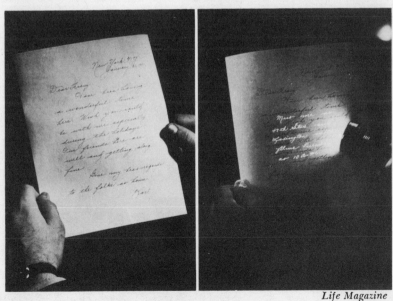

BETWEEN THE LINES OF A FRIENDLY NOTE, THE SPY HAS WRITTEN A
MESSAGE WITH INVISIBLE INK.

FRITZ DUQUESNE, HATER OF ENGLAND, CONVICTED GERMAN SPY, WHO MADE THE MISTAKE OF ADVERTISING HIS PROFESSION, POSED IN THE CHARACTER OF A FIELD MARSHAL——OR SOMETHING.

LILLY STEIN, GRADUATE OF A GERMAN SPY SCHOOL, WHOSE BEAUTY WAS HER STOCK IN TRADE BUT WHO SWAM INTO THE NET OF THE F.B.I.

power, he began setting down ship watchers and secret wireless stations on the shores of all the Americas. In troubled 1942 they gathered a rich harvest.

By an agreement reached long before World War II, military intelligence, the second organization under the supreme direction of Canaris, generally confined itself to Hitler's immediate objective: Europe; while the naval branch looked after the rest of the much desired globe. Contrary to the general impression, the professional or directing German spies detected in the United States have included few army officers. Those naval spies among us pried not only into ships, cargoes, and tactical plans for the fleets but into our military, aerial, and industrial preparations for war. In organizing this, his *corps d'élite*, Canaris followed the traditional British plan rather than the German one—quality rather than quantity, shoot with a rifle instead of a shotgun. This corps has been working as a unit almost since World War I. It has weeded out the incompetent agents, trained the competent to knife-edge keenness. Probably the core of the organization numbers no more than two or three hundred men. Of course these agents employ assistants, either paid informers among the native population, resident Germans, or such civilian graduates of the Naval School of Espionage at Hamburg as the chief may send them from time to time; but the underlings also are of high quality.

The third German agency for espionage has been a headache to Canaris. The Nazi party maintained from the first the *Auslander* Organization, or foreign section, which for practical purposes we may regard as identical with the foreign activity of the Gestapo. This large and industrious agency proceeded on the pretentious and illusive theory that every man with a drop of "the master blood" in him was not only in duty bound to support Germany in her rush toward world domination, but would with a little encouragement see his duty. When it began its work, Nicolai was still virtual director of German espionage and propaganda. He could never control these enthusiastic volunteers. However, before he turned them loose on us he persuaded them to modify their policy to a certain extent. They had cherished the illusion that "the thirty million people of Germanic blood" in the United States could be induced to start a civil war against "the Jew Rosenfeld." Nicolai, who remembered how miserably Papen's attempt at the same thing had failed in 1915, brought them back to earth. Germany, he submitted, could not count on the United States as an ally—at least not for the present. But by stirring up hatred of the Jews and distrust for England on the one hand and by appealing to our native love of peace on the other, she might hamper our manufacture of munitions for Britain and France and keep us from declaring war until it was too late for us to do anything effective.

The anti-Jewish literature that was flooding the country by 1938, the notorious German Bund and its alliance with the revivified Ku Klux Klan, the Silver Shirts and William Dudley Pelley and a hundred other fascist and even isolationist groups, *Social Justice* and Father Coughlin, George Sylvester Viereck—these activities belong to the story of German propaganda, which we are not telling here. But the *Auslander* was doing actual espionage and on a gigantic scale. The German Geopolitical Institute maintains an enormous reference library for the benefit of its fifth columns. During this disturbed period the Gestapo agents among us—German businessmen planted here for the purpose, German-Americans converted to the Nazi doctrine, hundreds of special consular employees, the eternal "tourists" and "students"—pried with Germanic thoroughness into our national defense, our geography, our industries, our capacity for production, our politics, our factions. They took or collected photographs with military meaning by the tens of thousands. They shipped whole carloads of material on German ships. In Berlin experts of the *Auslander* digested, filed, and indexed the reports. The files include, among other items, a gigantic "Who's Who in America" —room after room of notes on all our political, industrial, religious, educational, and artistic leaders, with special emphasis on their attitude toward the "New Europe."

"German espionage," the British Admiral Sir Reginald Hall has remarked, "is superficially clever and profoundly stupid." In such work as this, often the Germans cannot see the woods for the trees. They were laughing at us as a people so unsuspicious and communicative as to make us an easy mark for espionage, while they themselves were overlooking the freedom and enterprise of the American press. The Bund and other stooge organizations held rallies and promoted camps; and as early as 1934 our newspapers and magazines were introducing re-

porters among them and showing them up. In the preliminaries to World War I, the F.B.I. under Bruce Bielaski, together with the Secret Service, played a pair of
treys exceedingly well. But they had only a small force,
with limited legal sanction. Then, too, there was much
confusion as well as duplication of effort, since numerous
private and government agencies had their fingers in the
same pie. The Gestapo overlooked the fact that as World
War II approached, the work was co-ordinated under the
F.B.I., and that the powers of this organization over espionage and sabotage were extended. Complete coverage
was given to the Bund and the other dangerous organizations. Result: the Germans and German-Americans
whom the Gestapo were training for spies and saboteurs
among us became marked men when "the Day" dawned.
Some of them gave it up and left the country; most of
the rest went to internment camps within a month after
Pearl Harbor.

It was bungling, amateur work. But neither Nicolai
nor Canaris could do anything about it as yet—they belonged to the suspect old-officer class. However, when
Germany attacked Russia and Stalin promptly shot all of
the fifth columnists, Canaris struck with deadly speed.
He had been spying not only on the Russians but upon
the Gestapo agents. In a detailed report, he proved to
Hitler's satisfaction that their awkward work caused the
disaster. Forthwith, the Führer reorganized the foreign
section and put its espionage under the control of the
slippery admiral. However, the *Auslander,* in contrast
to naval intelligence, still works on the old German

theory of many agents and great risks of exposure—shooting with a shotgun instead of a rifle. One of its subsections recruits most of the new spies.

Long before he became co-ordinator of the whole system Canaris co-operated with Ribbentrop, once Ambassador to Britain, now Nazi Foreign Minister, in diplomatic espionage. Working well together, they organized those fifth columns which rendered conquest so easy in Poland, France, and Czechoslovakia. Most important to us, however, is the fact that they transformed the whole Nazi diplomatic service, embassies, legations, and consulates alike into a special service for espionage and propaganda.

The change, long on its way, became complete in 1938, when Germany had already seized Austria and the Sudetenland and played the comedy of "appeasement" with Chamberlain. Hitler recalled Hans Dieckhoff, an ambassador of the old school, from Washington and installed the suave, blond, Nazi-minded Hans Thomsen as chargé d'affaires. To the embassy at Washington, he added Baron von Gienanth, Adalbert Schoenwein, and Ernst Hepp. At the same time he shifted his personal aide, Captain Fritz Wiedemann, to the comparatively unimportant post of consul-general at San Francisco. And, finally, he removed the ambassador to Japan and put in his place General Eugen Ott, formerly the military attaché.

And every man jack of them was primarily a spy!

Hans Thomsen, chargé d'affaires, dowered with the powers and privileges of an ambassador, was an officer of naval intelligence, thoroughly trained through years of service.

Gienanth and Schoenwein belonged to the foreign service of the Gestapo, Heinrich Himmler's dreaded secret police. They took command of the wide Gestapo intelligence in the United States.

Hepp, hitherto correspondent for the Nazi news agency in the United States, had, of course, worked under the absolute command of Goebbels, Minister of Propaganda and Enlightenment. Now he took full charge of propaganda here and of fifth-column activities.

Ott, now ambassador at Tokio, was an officer of military intelligence.

Had we only known all the facts, we might have considered Wiedemann's appointment the most significant of all. In World War I, he had been captain of a German company that included a fanatical young corporal named Schicklgruber, alias Hitler. Like all natural criminals, Hitler has in his composition a wide streak of sentimentality. When he came to power, his associates said that Wiedemann was the only human being he held in reverence. He raised the obscure captain to a status equivalent to privy councillor. When Wiedemann bobbed up in San Francisco, the gossip columnists jumped to the conclusion that he had displeased Hitler and, having somehow dodged liquidation, departed into exile. A few San Franciscans interpreted it—and rightly—as a forecast of war in the Pacific; but only our intelligence officers perceived its real, immediate meaning. German and Japanese espionage, loosely linked since 1934, had entered into a close alliance; and Wiedemann in San Francisco was liaison officer between Hirohito's snoopers and Hitler's keyhole peepers.

It is no accident that the Japanese had organized their secret service on much the same pattern as the German —separate but co-ordinated army, navy, and diplomatic espionage with a large and loose amateur spy chain on the side.

For some years before the war of 1939, the German and Japanese intelligence departments, and to a certain extent the Italian, had a rough agreement. They exchanged useful information on the United States, and the Germans admitted Japanese students to their spy schools. The German missions then as now working in Japan include experts on espionage, sabotage, and psychological warfare, who lecture at the military colleges and give individual instruction to promising students. The dangerous, semicriminal Black Dragon Society which organized so many Japanese residents of the Pacific coast against us corresponds roughly to the Nazi party and the Gestapo. Again like the Germans, the Japanese used naval intelligence for the most important foreign jobs—all the more because everyone believed that sea power would determine any war between Japan and the United States. And after reaction triumphed in Japan and the army and navy took over the Empire, their embassy at Washington and their consulates everywhere were clearinghouses for espionage.

By contrast, even after Thomsen took charge in Washington, the German embassy avoided the appearance of having direct traffic in espionage. Our agencies of counterespionage have traced only two or three slight cases to its door. It was using the consulates as posts of command and as clearinghouses for espionage, especially the one in San Francisco under Wiedemann, and the Japanese embassy. Any really disagreeable job needing ambassadorial attention it shoved off onto the Japanese diplomats . . . history repeats itself, especially with the Germans. In 1915, when they were burning ships and blowing up factories at the rate of two a week, the German embassy moved Papen, its chief of espionage and sabotage, to New York and made the Austrian consulate its clearinghouse and "drop" for spy messages. There was a special reason in this case. The embassy had the important task of directing agitation against co-operation with Britain, of organizing the German-Americans into a pressure group. A spy scandal would have wrecked them.

What an era of popular blindness we had lived through! Even before World War I, the Japanese tourist with a mania for photography had become a joke on the Pacific coast; only the serious-minded noted that they were not wasting films on Yosemite Falls or Mount Whitney but were photographing such prosaic scenes as wharves, docks, warehouses, factories, and military reservations. As already stated, at a later period the Japanese fishermen of the Pacific coast were always making soundings off our coast and coast defenses, or hanging round the Pacific fleet when it conducted maneuvers. The authorities began to take notice; various Pacific states passed laws prohibiting alien ownership of seagoing vessels. Whereupon, the Japanese sold their ships to dummies and went cheerfully ahead.

Then in the middle 1930's, a purely criminal operation threw a lurid light on Japanese intentions toward us. One Yamamoto, boss gambler and Heaven knew what else, was the Japanese Al Capone of the Pacific coast. The Narcotic Squad of the Treasury Department had long been watching him. When after a long hunt for evidence it broke into his operations, it found that his drug ring was a gang of spies. Even in criminal opium smuggling the Japanese Government was their accomplice. The men who brought the drug across the Pacific traveled in immunity on Japanese liners; with the same immunity they served on the return voyage as couriers for Japanese naval intelligence. These boatmen in our harbors who performed the dangerous and difficult job of getting the opium ashore from the liners also put the gleanings of Japanese espionage aboard them. Yamamoto himself owned through dummies a fleet of thirty splendid motorboats that fished impartially for tuna, sea bass, and naval information. And so on. The public read of the Yamamoto case, with the opium feature played into the foreground, said "how interesting!" and forgot. The intelligence services of our government said nothing; but we know now that at about this time they began to take action with regard to the Japanese and German spy chains in our midst. For it was about that time that the case of Gunther Gustave Rumrich, *et al* called vivid attention to the fact that the Germans were using their merchant marine for similar purposes—and even more effectively.

It was a curious case, exceptional among modern spy operations for its melodramatic details. The first tip came from a postman in far-off Dundee, Scotland, who noticed that Mrs. Jesse Jordan, hairdresser and Scottish widow of a German killed in World War I, received an inordinate quantity of foreign mail. He notified the police. The British authorities, after gathering the evidence, arrested her as a spy and sent her up for four years. The search proved that among other treasonable acts she was "drop" for a spy ring operating in the United States and specializing on airplanes, coast fortifications, and naval plans. The British tipped off these facts to us; the F.B.I. went to work. They found that Rumrich, who afterward turned state's evidence, was the apparent head of the ring. German born, twice a noncommissioned officer and once a deserter in the United States Army, he had attended Bund meetings, gone violently Nazi, read Nicolai's works on the beauties of espionage, written to the colonel to offer his services, and so made contact with a German emissary through a "personal column" in the New York *Times*. The man who came to recruit him was a steward on the crack German liner *Europa;* and when Rumrich turned state's evidence, thereby getting off with a two-year sentence, he revealed an incredible situation in the German merchant marine. Every ship carried a kind of Nazi supercargo, usually disguised as a waiter or steward. He gave orders to the captain, who must obey his smallest whim—or else! On orders, the captain of the *Europa* carried from Germany the advertisement mentioned above, and saw that it was inserted in the *Times*. Other spies and couriers traveled on every trip, notably Johanna Hofmann, the *Europa's* hairdresser, who seemed to be chief of the courier service.

Rumrich gave good service while he lasted, for he had considerable ingenuity and inventiveness. He had been ordered to get the complete roster, with officers, of our troops in the New York area. Impersonating a major in the medical corps "who had to deliver a lecture in a hurry" he telephoned to headquarters asking for all the reports on venereal disease—and got them within an hour. Through his army experience, he knew that from these could be deduced the real information he wanted. Berlin had secured samples of White House notepaper and envelopes and counterfeited them. On these, Rumrich intended to write letters demanding secret documents and forge the President's signature to them. He had laid a plot to lure a certain colonel, carrying a bundle of most important documents, into a hotel room. There, two merry pirates of the *Europa's* crew were to knock the colonel cold with a narcotic and get away with the papers before he recovered. Happily, the F.B.I. had broken into the select circle by this time and a tip saved him.

Even prior to this time—in fact, in September, 1935— one William Lonkowski, a "piano tuner" of Brooklyn— really an agent for German military intelligence—forgot his technique. The *Europa* was at her dock waiting to sail eastward when he came aboard carrying a package—

contrary to port regulations—and was about to deliver it to Karl Schluter, who undoubtedly served as Hitler's supercargo on that ship, when the customs guards arrested him. The parcel and Lonkowski's pockets contained numerous documents which made it appear that he was possibly engaged in espionage activities. But all seemed to be "unrestricted"—not officially classified as secret. These, it was to appear later, came mostly from Otto Herman Voss, a mechanic in the Seversky plant, and from Eric Glaser, a private at Mitchel Field, army aviation headquarters for the New York area. These two were furnishing information to Rumrich also.

Here the story is blurred. Just why Lonkowski was allowed to return to his home is a matter not to be inquired into at present. At any rate, he went at once to his friend, Dr. Ignatz Griebl in Yorkville, who lent him a car in which he drove to Canada from whence he sailed back to Germany.

The popular, philandering Dr. Griebl, naturalized German who had become a reserve officer in the United States Army, seemed an important man in Nazi espionage against us; for a time, the government found, his residence was a clearinghouse for all Nazi espionage in the East. He furnished considerable information relative to Nazi activities and agreed to appear as a witness for the prosecution. Then for the first time the F.B.I. learned the details of a pleasant trip to Berlin. In June, 1937, he had sailed on the *Europa* with Miss Katherine Moog. En route, Schluter got acquainted with them, revealed himself for what he was, offered to take them to the heads of naval espionage in Hamburg and Berlin and made good his promise. Among others, Captain Udo von Bonin, one of masterspy Canaris' experts on American matters, entertained them and made propositions to them.

Griebl was to "spread the work" by securing highly placed agents in Washington. The plans for the fascinating and sophisticated Miss Moog were more piquant. She was to rent a large house at the capital, surround herself with other beauties, entertain lavishly—all at the expense of the "New Germany." Once established as a popular Bohemian hostess, she was to play for military and naval officers—frankly, to recruit them as informers and mercenary spies. "Their pay is miserably low," said one of the tempters in effect, "many of them are in debt. They will fall easily!"

Griebl appeared to have taken the hook, which was baited with some property confiscated from a Jew and the promise of a large sum to be delivered to him in Germany when he had finished his job. Miss Moog, who had no intention of accepting, played the game as only a clever woman can. Without committing herself, she left the impression that she had, and returned to New York where she did positively nothing for Germany and kept her mouth shut.

The F.B.I. recruited her and Griebl as witnesses. She testified at the trial, where Rumrich, Voss, Glaser, and Miss Hofmann drew sentences of from two to six years. But Griebl disappeared. Too late, the F.B.I. learned that he had sailed on the *Bremen* without ticket or passport. The ship was to touch land first at Cherbourg, France.

Our authorities notified the French police. They tried
to arrest him; but the captain, under orders from Schluter, refused to let them aboard. On he went to Berlin;
and to what eventual fate no one knows.

What happened on this ship is perhaps only a sample
of what was happening on every German ship in the
period of our careless neutrality. Intelligence material
was going to Berlin by carloads; American soldiers and
sailors are dying today because of the facts therein contained. And not only German ships. During the two
years before Hitler and Stalin went to war, communist-
minded seamen on Russian ships or vessels of neutral
registry carried messages which they delivered to German agents in European ports. The big German liners
carried the international mail; and testimony at the trial
of the ring on the *Europa* brought out the fact that Schluter, the Nazi steward and supercargo, used to pick the
locks of the bags containing mail for countries other than
Germany, look over the envelopes and steam open any
of them that seemed important. It is notable that among
them were letters bearing on the kind and quality of
munitions that Russia was buying in the United States.
And the German embassy pouches carried many important spy messages.

In this period we had among us another fifth column,
the agency being the Communist party and its fringe of
fellow travelers. There is proof of some old espionage for
the Soviet Government, notably in the Canal Zone. Also,
a few acts of naval sabotage, as when someone punctured
the insulation on a new cruiser, seem like communist

work. These, however, were perhaps the acts of irresponsible fanatics inspired by propaganda but acting on their own initiative. An odd episode happened in 1938, the "appeasement year." One of our federal agencies included several men who rated as fellow travelers. Blithely, it proposed a million-dollar project to photograph, map, and survey the state of development in all our defenses. Coastal forts, airfields, munitions factories, naval bases. German, Japanese, and Russian spies had been risking their liberty to get an imperfect picture of them. Now we proposed to do their work for the foreign spies and at our own expense! This may have been just starry-eyed innocence. But the project was officially approved, and only the vigilance of our naval intelligence prevented this, the biggest operation in autoespionage ever conceived in any country, from becoming a reality.

However, up to the outbreak of World War II, the American communists were less concerned with espionage and mere physical sabotage than with propaganda and mental sabotage. Following the old communist motto, "Break down that we may build on the ruins," they developed an original and most effective technique. Whenever Americans formed a society to promote any liberal or advanced cause such as ameliorating the lot of shopgirls, aiding the Spanish Republic, or dealing with unemployment, the party wormed a few communists into it. While the merely liberal majority worked at the job only in their spare time, the busy communists worked twelve hours a day; and presently the organization changed from white to pale pink to blush rose to deep red. They wormed into the labor unions, where they often wrought the same transformations. They established "cells" in the army and especially in the navy and distributed red and seditious literature to the rank and file. One intelligence agent who had worked his way into the party reported that at a secret meeting two members announced that they were officers in the United States Army—one a captain and one a major. And so on. It was effective work—so effective that later the Germans, in their propaganda designed to keep the United States from aiding the Allies, copied it almost slavishly. The communists were bursting their veins with bawling denunciation of fascism, including the German brand. At the same time, they raised the cry of "imperialist war" against France and Britain. And so they supported the neutrality bill as later they opposed the Cash and Carry Act.

These activities carried them across the line between propaganda and sabotage. Intermittent outlaw strikes in American factories manufacturing munitions for Britain marked this period. They lost millions of man-hours to the cause so soon to be our own. German money inspired some of them, no doubt, but communist boring from within many more.

Stalin, who had never taken our communists here into his confidence, knocked the wind out of them by signing his nonaggression treaty with Germany. There followed the invasion of Poland and her partition between Stalin and Hitler. Getting their wind back, the communists limited their denunciation of fascism to American and

British capitalists and co-operated heartily in the German effort to keep us out of this "capitalist war." While the Germans worked on the white-collar class and the German-American population, the communists took care of the "overall" class. Even though we ourselves were arming furiously, the inspired strikes in munitions plants by no means stopped. Of all the agencies opposing the draft and trying to break down army morale, communists were most industriously effective. Constantly, circulars and pamphlets urging soldiers to repudiate the "imperialist war" reached the hands of American soldiers. They planted agents—often women—in the honky-tonks surrounding army camps, and even in the U.S.O. And as a climax, they placed "peace pickets" before the White House.

Few of the German and Japanese spy plots exposed between 1938 and 1942 involved American communists. Like the German embassy, they were doing work too valuable to be ruined by any implication like that. But they helped occasionally. We have mentioned the red courier service not only on Russian cargo ships but also on neutral vessels employing Russian sailors. And our counterintelligence knows now that their agents sometimes passed to the German spymasters any good piece of military information that came their way. Also once a set of communists tried to bribe their way to a look at the files of naval intelligence on the Pacific coast.

Hitler took his turn at punching the American communists in the solar plexus when on June 22, 1941, and almost out of a clear sky, he added Stalin to his sucker list and turned the blitzkrieg loose on Russia. For a moment our reds were the comedy relief in a cosmic tragedy. Up to the day when the guns began to shoot, the New York *Daily Worker,* official party organ, had been denouncing the "capitalist war," attacking "British imperialism," beseeching America to keep out of the mess. For a day and a night the *Daily Worker* sat on the fence while a "bourgeois" New York newspaper telephoned every hour to ask the editor a single monotonous question: "Have you got your orders from Moscow yet?" Then the party and the newspaper, executing another abrupt about-face, turned from isolationist to interventionist, withdrew their pickets from the White House, substituted war rallies for peace parades, and helped sincerely in all our military preparations. More pertinent to this book is the fact that they peached on their former acquaintances in the German secret services. All around, the communists became model soldiers both in deed and example and now co-operate nobly in keeping watch on espionage and against sabotage in shipping and industry.

In those years of waiting and dreading the inevitable, both espionage and counterespionage in the United States grew constantly more intense. Of counterespionage we shall treat in another chapter. We have already touched on the main German operations that came to light, such as the Ludwig-Osten case, the Duquesne case, the Japanese rings that recruited Farnsworth and Thompson. At least one other formidable Japanese ring was snooping and prying into our naval secrets. In Japanese espionage, the Naval Association corresponds roughly to the German *Auslander* organization. When it comes to aims and objectives, its constitution scarcely minces matters. The association, it declares, exists to "investigate" and "report on" naval vessels and bases in foreign ports. For at least ten years before Pearl Harbor, Dr. Takaashi Furusawa, its president, lived in Los Angeles. He had a sanitarium, many of whose patients were Japanese naval officers ashore from ships in San Pedro Harbor. When, a day or two after Pearl Harbor, we interned him, the authorities said that this place was the clearinghouse for Japanese espionage on the Pacific coast. In 1938, one of our secret services reported that 138 agents in California were reporting to Japan every day by radio; and the number did not decline in the three years before Pearl Harbor.

At long last, we began to put naval docks, bases, and yards under a tight guard. But the Japanese "tourists" with their little cameras found ways to beat this precaution. "They seeped through like water," said a man who commanded one of these guards, "catch them at it and they said 'so sorry—regrettable mistake!' Pinch them, and they got off with a light fine or a reprimand." For in spite of new laws, we were going easy on Japanese espionage. The situation, Washington felt, was so ticklish that an unfortunate "incident" might precipitate a useless war. The Japanese naval officers who were the procurers and paymasters of such treasonable informers as Farnsworth and Thompson were allowed quietly to sail home. In one Pacific coast city, the Japanese set up the equivalent of Stieber's infamous Green House in Berlin—an establishment to which spy recruiters lured weak sisters in the services, photographed them in compromising positions, and tried to blackmail them into taking the black shilling. And nothing could be done about it except to put this place most strictly out of bounds for all officers and men of the United States Army and Navy. A Japanese drove up to a remote spot on the coast of Florida and prepared to photograph one of our naval vessels. "So sorry!" he said when arrested. "So sorry" said the government when we found that he was a Japanese diplomat; and the judge let him go.

Then Pearl Harbor. And the next week, we struck and continued to strike. With a sureness that proved how efficiently the F.B.I. and the intelligence departments of the army and navy had been working, we interned hundreds of Germans, Italians, and a few odds and ends of other nationalities as dangerous enemy aliens. In the first fourteen months of the war thirty-four such were interned for the duration. Following which, we moved out or interned virtually all the Japanese on the endangered Pacific coast.

Among the Germans were many who were suspected of spying, and scores of others established in technical and key positions, all set to begin work as soon as we went to war. The Italians were mostly profascist agitators. Although Mussolini maintained his paid propagandists here, only a handful of his henchmen in the United States were ever caught spying; and they were mostly in the employ of Germany. As for the Japanese, while a large proportion of the "Nisei" or native born are as thoroughly American as any Smith, Jones, or Casey, we could take no chances with the entanglements of Oriental psychology. When, a few months later, the eight saboteurs landed from a submarine's rubber boat and Herbert Karl Fredrich Bahr was picked up among the diplomats and refugees returning on the *Drottningholm,* the public carefully assumed that they had been driven to these extraordinary devices by the completeness of our countermeasures—that the spy menace was over.

Our authorities know that only by eternal vigilance can spies be detected and either kept under surveillance or arrested. The situation is as well under control as a matter so elusive as espionage in a democracy as big as this ever can be.

It can hardly be literally true that "good spies don't get caught," but in many of the spy rings we have uncovered, one or more members has given himself away through bad technique. "Those idiotic Yankees!" wrote Franz von Papen to his wife. The gang operating on the *Europa* seemed to be guided by the same motto. Dr. Griebl was a man marked as a violent Nazi propagandist; he was one of the first residents of Yorkville whom the federal police watched as a potential spy. If Fritz Duquesne had lettered on his door SPY AGAINST ENGLAND, he would not have advertised his profession and intentions more openly than he had done during forty years of self-sought publicity. When by promises and threats agents of the Gestapo recruited Sebold in Germany, they failed correctly to judge his character and American loyalty; else they would have known that when they sent him as a spy to an American consulate to apply for a passport, he would enlist under the Stars and Stripes as a counterspy.

On the other hand, the Germans may have formed some of these rings of inept, dumb, and conspicuous spies as red herrings in order to distract attention from the work of better spies on the same job. That is an old trick of European espionage. Captain Ulrich von der Osten was a trained professional who operated as far back as World War I. He worked not with the brutal, heavy-handed and amateurish Gestapo, but under the expert German naval intelligence—possibly under Canaris himself. But for the accident, fortunate for us, in which a taxicab killed him, he might be working yet, free and unsuspected. All during 1942 the newspapers told us that the F.B.I. had rounded up this or that set of enemy aliens with radio transmitters and firearms in their possession; we learned little of their subsequent fate. Some of them were willing amateurs looking for a chance, others were small spies who, even if they confessed, could tell nothing except their own operations and the assumed names of the men who employed and paid them. No more than you or I could they name the big and really dangerous spy at the head of the ring. When German and Italian submarines were operating near our own shores, ships went down because of information sent to the German or Italian submarines by shore-based radio. Our watchers of the ether are still picking up fragments of messages in cipher and code. We had been at war nearly a year when someone discovered that the telephone wire into an important military office had been tapped. Our military detectives ran down the tap wire and the men who did the job were arrested. Two of them were Italians—which is unusual.

Now that the Japanese are interned, now that the Bund is dead, now that we keep a strict watch on every passenger landing from abroad, now that 95 per cent of the German-American element on whom Hitler counted so optimistically are playing ball with Uncle Sam, where do Japanese intelligence and Admiral Canaris get their spies?

Doubtless a few German spies of the professional class —intelligence officers and graduates of the spy schools— are still seeping into the United States. Although our blimps have made our Atlantic coast most unsafe for submarines, there is no perfect guarantee that more spies have not landed by the route of the eight saboteurs. However, in 1943 as in 1914–18 the Mexican border is still the probable route. Our southern neighbor is sincerely in the war on our side. But it is a thinly settled country, poorly provided with communications. In some districts dwell Indian tribes so primitive that they cannot even speak Spanish. Counterespionage against a foreign enemy is to the Mexican Government a new activity and the navy is so small that even to the end of the war it may never be able perfectly to guard the wild Mexican coasts.

Further, in the years of Hitler's preparation for global war, more and more Germans drifted into Mexico. Most of them founded legitimate businesses and settled there. Of course they were serving Hitler. In a country so wild as Mexico, getting to the northern border is not difficult for a resourceful man. Crossing the border—well, in spite of increased precautions, it can be managed. Such spies always have their papers in perfect order; all intelligence services employ experts to forge passports, draft-registration cards, and other "proofs" of false identity. There were Japanese colonies in Mexico. They have suddenly shrunk in size. Where have the absentees gone? Surely not back to Japan! Some Japanese can pass as Indians; and Mexican counterespionage suspects that in wild country along the coast they are giving aid, comfort, and information to Axis submarines.

Mexico is a focus of another ticklish situation. The Spanish Falangistas, prop of Franco's one-party rule, are as nationalistic and totalitarian as the German Nazis, and are organized in much the same fashion. Their Falangist Council of Hispanidad is a Spanish version of the German *Auslander*. It holds that every man of Spanish blood in the world owes his first allegiance to Spain and its new order; that every nation carved from the old empire of Philip II must eventually be won back to the motherland. That would include the Philippines, Porto Rico, and Cuba. Ever since Franco overthrew the Spanish Republic, the Falangists have been operating on the same plan as the Nazis—stirring up and recruiting fanatics of Spanish blood in Latin America and the Orient, spreading its central doctrine, "World leadership is Spain's birthright." Before Cuba woke up, it operated there a passport and visa mill and a radio station for the benefit of its agents. Across the world in the Philippines the Falangists operated through the *Ganap*—which loyal

Filipinos call "the Gang." Anti-American and anti-Quezon, it favors a totalitarian government, under Japanese backing, in the Philippines. In spite of the large Japanese population, there was little or no sabotage in Honolulu during the attack on Pearl Harbor, whereas during the battle at Manila there was a great deal; and the Filipinos lay these jobs to the *Ganap* as much as to the Japanese residents. In South and Central America up to 1942, many of the Spanish diplomats followed the totalitarian pattern of diplomacy by serving as centers of espionage. But when victory began to swing toward the United Nations, Madrid reorganized its diplomatic corps in the Americas and called home the men most notable for sympathy with the Axis.

The Falangists were especially active in Mexico. There, they worked with the Sinarcistas, a semisecret society that made its first appearance in Yucatán but is now most active along the Rio Grande. Except for the Spain-over-all idea, it does not differ in political principle from the Falangist organization. Both are profascist, pro-Axis, anticommunist, anti-Jew, anti-Mason, antidemocratic. They differ from the northern totalitarians, however, in their views on religion. With both, support of the Roman Catholic Church is a cardinal doctrine.

The Falangists had an active organization in the United States before Pearl Harbor. Then it disbanded —officially. Actually, it simply sank out of sight. The Sinarcistas have been sneaking across the Mexican border to distribute rabid fascist literature among the Spanish-speaking residents of our Southwestern states.

Some of this stuff has even shown up in Harlem, New York City; they, like the Japanese before Pearl Harbor, are playing for our Negro population. So are the Filipino *Ganap*, who have branches in New York, Chicago, and San Francisco. Indeed, it is known that when the Japanese diplomats had to go home and most of the other Japanese residents were put out of harm's way, they turned over much of their espionage in the United States to one or another of these societies. These spies are in a very pleasant position. We are at peace with Spain. So Spanish vessels enter and leave our ports without let or hindrance. It is virtually impossible perfectly to guard against a courier service on neutral ships. We are in regular communication with South America by airplane. An air-mail letter from New York will reach any capital city on that continent in two or three days. Again, it is virtually impossible for our censorship to treat every letter on suspicion of invisible ink. So messages of use to the Axis go through to fake addresses; thence a ship or a short-wave radio apparatus in some remote part of that thinly settled continent takes them in cipher to Berlin or Tokio. Commissions from Spain still range this country looking into our agricultural and industrial methods. Nothing prevents one of their members, if he so wills, from looking into more important things; and it is notable that one German arrested on suspicion of espionage was caught in the act of trying to smuggle out a letter to the Spanish embassy at Washington.

Before Pearl Harbor, the Germans were playing for support, aid, and comfort not only from people of "the master blood" in the United States, but from Hungarians, Croats, Ukrainians, and Rumanians. They failed to understand the pull of America on the immigrant of European blood. When the pinch came, these people stood by the new country. The Germans had counted on help in America from the Irish Republican Army, that outlaw element as distasteful to the government of Eire as to us. Also, Father Coughlin's *Social Justice* had revived in many Irish-Americans the old hatred of England. Before Pearl Harbor, indeed, men of the I.R.A. element did us some actual damage, and planned even more. If the Germans counted on disloyalty among the Irish after Pearl Harbor, they failed to understand the spirit of a fighting race. Two months later, Kelly and Burke and Shea were back on our casualty lists—as were Müller and Schmitz and Schwartz. And the agents of the Irish Republican Army diverted their energies to spying on our troops in North Ireland and attempting to subvert their loyalty.

Yet there are a hundred and thirty million of us; among them born criminals, lone wolves, perverse natures. That 5 per cent of the German-Americans with divided loyalties mostly take it out in wishing that Hitler might win or at least get an even break. Only a few of them would risk life or liberty for his cause. The prompt execution of the six saboteurs and the conviction of the parents who harbored and abetted one of them have proved that Uncle Sam will tolerate no more fooling. And on the ones who have spat out their feelings, there is a close watch. Yet men and women who have never uttered a disloyal word in public may be performing the most disloyal acts of all acts in private. So may fascist-minded individuals among the Hungarians, Rumanians, Ukrainians, Croats, and so on. Open professions of loyalty may be only a screen. One of the most effective spies in history, Ievno Azeff, sat in the inner councils of the Russian nihilists and betrayed every plot that they formed to the Czarist secret police.

Quislings high and low made easier the conquest of Norway, Denmark, Holland, and Belgium, all maritime nations. A good part of their ships escaped and took service in the hard, heroic task of ferrying American supplies to the United Nations. In spite of British vigilance, the Germans have planted Quislings in some of their crews. Jumping ship at New York or Boston for a turn at espionage in the United States is not impossible. The Gestapo blackmails Germans into espionage by threatening to abuse or even kill their relatives; it has at least tried this same device against loyal sailors on these ships. We hear only of the failures; we may never hear of instances where this brutal threat accomplished its purpose.

After France fell and the Vichy Government became a virtual ally of Germany, the rather small French element in the United States split into two camps. The larger and more articulate supported the Free French with meetings, funds, and propaganda; but a silent and affluent minority favored Vichy and "collaboration." Whether they gave more active help no one knows; the obscure and delicate game the State Department was playing with Vichy prevented close inquiry. But all that time, French steamers were carrying Axis agents be-

tween Marseilles, Martinique, and South America; while
the West Indies were a hotbed of espionage for the benefit of German submarines. When Admiral Darlan fled to
North Africa and co-operated in our landing, this element seemed to swing toward the side of the United Nations. Then came Darlan's assassination and the virtual
refusal of the Free French to co-operate with anyone who
had collaborated with Vichy; and the situation became
obscure again.

Before we entered the war, American fascists like
Pelley and Christians were helping Hitler by violent,
abusive propaganda; they represented a disturbingly
large element. Some of their publications went further.
With malice aforethought, they supplemented the work
of Hitler's spies by supplying information of distinct
military value. First, they gave Dr. Goebbels cues on
exploitable rifts in our unity and morale; and he did exploit them. Second, into merely abusive articles on our
government and its preparations to further the "Jewish
plot," they inserted choice bits of information on our
more or less secret military preparations. Through the
Axis consulates and embassies, through stooges in neutral countries, they took pains to see that every page of
this material reached Berlin, Rome, or Tokio. This
also applies to some subversive "newsletters" garnered
and forwarded by such camouflaged enemy agencies as the
Mitsui Company in New York. These people did not
simply shoot a poisoned arrow into the air to fall to
earth they knew not where—they damned well aimed it.

Most of this noisy lot are silenced or in jail. But how

many of their unknown partners are still working underground? Since unbalanced characters filled with sensational, biased literature tend to transform thought into action, their propaganda was a kind of recruiting agency for spies. Influenced by such literature as this, a young crackpot radio "ham" in 1942 offered to transmit military information to Germany and did send a message prepared by a "German spy" who had accepted his offer—and who proved to be an F.B.I. agent. Counterespionage officers in one important area regularly ask suspected saboteurs, "Do you read *Social Justice?*" And one of the authors heard a man who had set fire to an army pier answer, "Yes."

The communists, the Nazis, and the Japanese, in turn, have played on the wrongs of the Negro. When the Japanese "diplomats" withdrew from among us they left behind them a Negro-Moslem congregation in Chicago, committed to their aims, and a Negro society in Harlem dedicated to the proposition: "A colored world under leadership of Japan." Local and federal authorities have squelched these uprisings, but that is no guarantee that a few Negroes, victimized by Japanese buncombe, are not spying. Still Japan, in contrast with Germany, is rather poorly off for spy material in the United States. Some of our federal police believe that after Pearl Harbor our two supreme enemies entered into an agreement on secret service. In return for favors in other fields, they think, Japan dropped espionage in our continental area, leaving the field to the Germans who were to share with their allies the material they gathered. It is also reported that the Germans are holding out the choicest bits. That would be entirely in character.

Finally, we must not overlook the possibility of informers, even informers in high places. If that is not happening, it is the first time any nation ever escaped such treason in a serious war. Any patriot who disbelieves this should read Carl Van Doren's *Secret History of the American Revolution* and learn how many who passed as prominent and loyal Americans were secretly in the pay of the British General Clinton. Some of these informers might be the most dangerous spies of all.

The actual professional spies in the United States may number only a few hundred—though including amateurs there may be a few thousand—among a hundred and thirty millions. And most if not all of them are spotted. But here, figures are illusive. In the proper conditions, one spy is enough to win a battle or a campaign. Remember Mrs. Greenhow's message to General Beauregard. Remember Belle Boyd emerging mysteriously from a wood to give Stonewall Jackson exactly the information he needed in order to drive General Banks out of the Shenandoah. And just imagine that a highly placed spy had found, and transmitted to the Germans in advance, General Eisenhower's plans for invading North Africa!

CHAPTER FIVE

THE SPYHUNT: COUNTER-ESPIONAGE

ANYONE even superficially versed in military affairs knows the great advantage accruing to the side that holds the initiative. In totalitarian war, the spy has this advantage to a supreme degree. One active spy may keep thousands of counteragents busy—censors, border guards, government detectives, military and naval police, local police, organizations so secret that they have no name. Indeed, German writers on total espionage have listed this among the advantages of their system. It causes a wholesale diversion of men and women who might be fighting at the front or producing munitions.

When, nearly a century ago, Germany's Stieber plus conscription forced organized espionage in peace as well as in war upon continental Europe, all the nations involved had perforce to create a system of permanent counterespionage. Government in that truculent area was centralized to a degree that Americans have never known, even in war. Not only did the capitals organize forces of secret police with extraordinary powers, but they had their hands on the smallest village constable. Spyhunting became as much the business of any policeman as the search for forgers and murderers. Even in

France, which granted to citizens and visitors more personal liberty than most of the others, no hotel sheltered a stranger without notifying the police of his name, occupation, and business in town. All this constituted a preliminary training for a counterespionage which became effective as soon as the nation declared war.

Russia carried this system to the extreme. A large, powerful, and tyrannical body of secret police called the Ochrana propped the wobbly throne of the Czars. Existing primarily to guard the monarchy against internal rebellion, it also watched for spies from without. The Ogpu (now N.K.V.D.) of the U.S.S.R. is merely the heir of the Ochrana. It is more efficient, however; and it draws additional strength from the fact that it has behind it and assisting it the Communist party. Hitler stole this system, lock, stock, and barrel. Gradually the German Gestapo, corresponding to the Ogpu, acquired dictatorial powers second only to Hitler's own. "Hangman" Heydrich, whom the Czechs informally executed for his cruelties, perfected counterespionage against both domestic dissenters and foreign spies. His was the idea of the *Blockwarte*, a counterspy with power of search, seizure, and snooping in every city block; his the slimy creation of the *Volksmeldedienst*, a universal tattletale service aiding the Gestapo. Heydrich is gone, but his system lives on. It is effective. Intelligence officers have estimated that in spite of an active underground, we get 70 per cent less reliable information from Germany than in the previous war. As for Japan, such methods against dissenters and foreigners were always flesh of her flesh.

Manifestly, the democracies, even in total war, cannot adopt such drastic and barbarous methods without surrendering their souls to the enemy. Any attempt to do so would only disrupt our morale. Except during the period preceding our entry into the two World Wars, Americans have never known even the shadow of organization for counterespionage; in those periods of crisis we were forced to improvise. If between 1914 and 1917 our measures were imperfect, the fault lies with a Congress that would never grant sufficient funds nor pass adequate laws, rather than with the two organizations having much power to act in the emergency—the Federal Bureau of Investigation, Department of Justice, under Bruce Bielaski and the Secret Service of the Treasury Department under William J. Flynn.* When they stopped the German practice of putting firebombs on ships bearing munitions for the Allies, when they made America too hot to hold such German spy-diplomats as Albert, Papen, Boy-Ed and Dumba, they had often to slip through some very thin loopholes in the law. Fortunately, they had able assistance from British naval intelligence, from the secret corps of Czechoslovak counterspies organized by E. V. Voska, and from similar societies among the other rebellious races subject to the Germans and Austrians. Largely because Bielaski and Flynn were

* The specific name, Secret Service, given to this bureau, should not be confused with the generic term secret service used to describe all forms of detective work for governments. The F.B.I. and American military and naval intelligence perform secret service, but they are not a part of the United States Secret Service.

able detectives, they did miraculously well considering that they were fighting in handcuffs.

When about 1938 history began to repeat itself, we were in a much stronger position. Army and navy intelligence, virtually nonexistent in 1914 but most efficient organizations by 1918, did not utterly let down after the Armistice. For twenty years they maintained among the reserve officers an intelligence department whose members went to school to learn this odd trade. The plans of both services included methods for expanding intelligence work as soon as war broke out or became imminent. Finally, the epidemic of bank robberies, kidnapings, and gang murders which marked our late prohibition era, and, when the country went wet again, the adjustment of the gangsters to new criminal trades, led Congress to build up the F.B.I. through liberal appropriations and to pass new laws giving it greater powers to detect and arrest interstate criminals.

From this lurid episode, J. Edgar Hoover emerged as the most eminent policeman in the world and his F.B.I. the best force of detective police. It would be superfluous to describe in detail the high standards of education, character, and training that the F.B.I. has set for its personnel, the unprecedented percentage of its cases that end with a conviction, its employment and improvement of all known scientific methods for detecting crime, its efficient shooting when shooting becomes necessary. Schoolboys who could not pass an examination on the Supreme Court or the Cabinet can tell you all about the

F.B.I. But one point deserves stress. Ever since Hoover began to perfect it, he has worked to educate municipal and state police officials in modern methods of detection, and to build up co-operation among law-enforcement agencies throughout the country.

When about 1935 the Bund and other German-inspired organizations became perniciously active, the F.B.I. went to work, identified for future reference the chief German agents among them, and began its own education in counterespionage. For one thing, almost every agent on the force had to take a special course in the art of detecting espionage. And when in 1940 the German air force loosed its blitz on London, agents from Washington went to London to study police methods for handling the populace during air raids—and other wartime contingencies.

Steadily it went on from there—the *Europa* ring, the Duquesne ring, the Ludwig ring, and other cases, many of which never reached the newspapers. By the time we entered the war, Mr. Hoover himself and the agents under him had with admirable fluidity learned the difference between crime detection and military counterespionage. The force comprised by now almost five thousand agents. Further, it had been instructing the municipal, county, and local police in counterintelligence work and arranging close co-ordination with them. The entrance requirements of character, clean record, and intelligence still stood; but the old requirements of a law degree or a license in accountancy were relaxed to admit men with academic degrees, command of foreign languages, or extensive experience in investigation work.

Finally, while isolationists and interventionists were still having it out and Japan was tricking us with "peace missions," the Administration designated the F.B.I. as leader and co-ordinator of domestic spyhunting in liaison with military and naval intelligence. Amateur spyhunters are not wanted; this is no war for tyros. When the Japanese attacked Pearl Harbor, one department of our counterespionage was trained and ready.

But only one department. Hunting down spies or foiling their efforts is not the whole scope of counterespionage. Equally important in a literate democracy is preventing the periodical press and the average citizen from carelessly passing on information to the enemy. In countries like Germany which have installed total counterespionage, censorship and propaganda lie under the control of one bureau. Rightly so, perhaps; the two activities interlock in a manner which only the expert can appreciate. When we entered the war, these activities were scattered around through six or eight federal organizations that were wasting much motion through duplicated work, sheer ignorance, and lack of any clear policy. Giving ear to the roars of the newspapers, the President consolidated and reorganized them under the new Office of War Information, with Elmer Davis in general command and the Office of Censorship, with Byron Price directing. Over all foreign communications, the censorship has in practice almost as much authority as obtains in any totalitarian country. As for the periodical press, the newspapers and magazines had already set up a voluntary censorship of their own, in full co-operation with government agencies. Stories, articles, and books are not censored in detail except by special request; the O.W.I. or the Office of Censorship merely inform the editors from time to time on the kind of matter they should not print because it might give aid and comfort to the enemy.

The Federal Communications Commission, which licenses and regulates radio and has power over telegraph and cable lines, had been working with the F.B.I. ever since it began to track down the transmitting stations of German spies. When the first bomb of our war woke the country from its dream of isolation, the F.C.C. was already in its stride and had imposed a close censorship, under military advice, on foreign cables, short-wave radio stations and domestic stations. In 1940 we passed a law requiring all aliens to register and to carry certificates of identity—a measure most useful to any policeman tracking down potential spies.

That, plus the unofficial help of the public in general, is the setup for detecting spies among civilians of the United States. Let us now consider the methods and principles of counterespionage.

Military authorities mostly agree that the most useful and important agency for keeping the enemy from learning about military preparations and intentions is the least dramatic one—censorship over the printed word, the written or telegraphed word, even the spoken word. It is also the one most irksome to the average citizen, especially the American. But it is absolutely necessary in modern war, and the only difference of opinion concerns its extent.

In totalitarian countries like Germany and Japan, which have always been regimented, the government agent can seize and open domestic letters, set a censor beside every telegraph key and suppress newspapers without rousing indignation or suspicion in the public. Not so with the democracies. During the first year of World War I, France and Britain tried the experiment of conducting a war without war correspondents. The public was supposed to satisfy itself with a brief, colorless, and often deliberately inaccurate communiqué. As regards treatment of the war in general, in Britain the army issued general orders to the newspapers which they ignored on peril of a long term in jail for the responsible editor. In France, a censor stood over every editor and, when the paper was put to bed, lifted paragraphs and columns of type from the forms so that the finished product was spotted with suggestive blank spaces. However, the government could not stop the mouths of soldiers home on leave. They filled in the blanks—with a deplorable effect on civilian morale. The French and British, seeing the light at last, began in the second year to admit correspondents to their lines and to censor their stories at field headquarters. That became universal practice for democracies at war, including ours. In this war, however, censorship is usually so much more lenient that it has been said that the aim seemed to be not to mystify enemy intelligence officers by telling them nothing, but to drive them crazy by telling them everything—true and untrue.

Yet this is only a compromise. In all democracies, and especially in the United States which has enjoyed the freest press in the world, there is a no man's land of strife and struggle between maintenance of military secrecy and maintenance of civilian morale. Daily, the intelligence experts of our armed forces read in their newspapers little items that make them shudder; for these are the trifles that the enemy's intelligence experts may use to build up a picture. Down in Texas, a bluejacket home on leave tells the newspapers about a naval battle long past. So does a gunner's mate in California and an aviator in Ohio. The enemy expert compares these stories. He is like one of those paleontologists who, given four or five fossil bones of an extinct animal, can reproduce the whole skeleton. From common factors, he can perhaps describe for the Japanese a piece of American naval battle tactics that has been baffling them.

The mere appearance at a given place of several American soldiers from a definite division may give the expert the cue to a military movement. In 1942, the censors requested the newspapers not to publish the statistics of mild epidemics, such as measles, in local training camps. This seemed captious. It was not. Medical statistics show the percentage of men likely to be infected with such an epidemic. A little multiplication, and a spy would have the approximate number of men in the camp. The same rule applies even more aptly to our production of munitions. To say of certain small items that the enemy would find them out anyway is not valid criticism. One object of counterespionage—as of espionage—is to keep the opponent busy, to do its bit to wear down his energies.

At least twice during the vital year 1942, American publications innocently handed the enemy not mere fragments of information but the complete product. In one case, a periodical published a beautiful panoramic night photograph of the lighted war factories along the Detroit River. Had Germany intended to attack Detroit with bombers from a carrier, this would have been as useful to her as the combination of the safe to a burglar. Again: a returned correspondent, freed from censorship at the source, wrote a "now-it-can-be-told" story of a battle. He was a good reporter and, in this case, unfortunately accurate. Also, his act violated no law. But the story got back to the enemy—proving that spies are still working in this country—and gave them valuable information.

On the other hand, shall we impose upon every newspaper office a censor instructed to pare every military or naval item to the bone? That, as all experts on the American press know, would pour cold water on the hot fires of patriotism. In late 1942 and early 1943, censorship in North Africa suppressed all intelligent and revealing reference to the political muddle among the French. Every American newspaper reader knows the result— violent partisanship, hot letters to the editor, injury to our confidence in the State Department and even in General Eisenhower. Perhaps this silence was necessary in order to guard military intentions; but the effect was a state of mind which the enemy tries hard to produce.

A wholly controlled and censored press serving a people to whom the bread and meat of news have become a necessity would only result in our eating the husks and offal of rumor.

Drawing the line between strict military secrecy and keeping our people from going sour on the war is in the nature of an art; and not every man with qualifications as a censor is an artist. So there have been gross blunders here and there; but so far, our voluntary censorship of the periodical press has worked reasonably well in important matters. In spite of the liberty of expression granted our press, we deceived the Germans as to the objectives of our expedition to North Africa. When in January, 1943, Roosevelt and Churchill held their historic conference at Casablanca, the Germans seem to have had a dim idea that their chief enemies were meeting somewhere; but they set the scene in London. Scores of Americans, including many newspapermen, knew our intentions in both cases; yet not a word leaked into the press or into the ears of any German spy.

Censorship at the source of news has worked more effectively. What a reporter does not know will not be written. In all military camps, in all bureaus and departments of the army and navy at Washington, and of course in all army headquarters and fleets operating abroad, serve expert public-relations officers, many of them trained newspapermen who know all the tricks. They give out such news as is considered safe for the public to know, answer or parry the questions of reporters, assist them to get harmless but helpful information. This system extends even to those munitions establishments which private capital is operating under supervision of the government. Some, no reporter ever enters. Others he enters only on his promise to "lay off" certain features, to work under escort of an officer, and to submit his copy for censorship. Our economic war agencies at Washington take similar precautions.

The eternal problem of espionage is communications. The spy must get his news through to his own army and navy. Further, as emphasized before, time is an important factor. Let us imagine that an American spy sent on December 3, 1941, a message revealing the Japanese movement on Pearl Harbor. Had it arrived on December 6, it would have saved the day for us; but say that it arrived on December 9, when we were cleaning up the ruins! This necessity for speed sometimes drives the spy to take desperate chances. Hence, our sixteen thousand civilian censors, dealing mostly with cables, short-wave wireless stations, and foreign mails, not only make espionage much more difficult but catch spies. The "perfect" system, as applied in Germany, implies an equally strict watch over domestic mails and telegraph offices. Such censorship would not only run contrary to American ideas, but it would be nearly impossible to enforce in a country so large and literate. Here, our counterspies work under a handicap. The federal agent looking for spies has no more legal right to pick another man's letter out of the domestic mails and steam it open than has an overcurious private citizen. This immunity of the domestic mails is the chief leak in our censorship. There is nothing to prevent a spy in California or Oregon from sending his information by air mail or common post to a confederate with a short-wave wireless apparatus in New Jersey—or to an American town on the Mexican border across which, despite precaution, it may be smuggled.

Another brake on American counterespionage the Supreme Court imposed at an unfortunate time—the eve of war. This pertained to wire tapping. If in October or November, 1941, the F.B.I. and the intelligence officers of our services had been able to tap the telephone wires of the 250 "attachés" of the Japanese consulate at Honolulu, we might have averted the disaster at Pearl Harbor. Now, however, by specific permission of the Attorney General, federal agents may tap wires in cases involving grave danger to national security.

The foreign mails and telegraphic communications are the bottleneck; and censorship on them is close and severe, especially as regards letters to and from neutral Europe and South America. At the building which is the largest knot in our web of censorship one sees only a series of tables with men in their shirt sleeves working on piles of letters. Each table represents a language; out of our foreign-born population, whose loyalty in this crisis has proved one of our strengths, we have drawn censors in nearly a hundred tongues, from Armenian along the alphabet to Yiddish.

But postal censors must be more than expert linguists. This work requires something akin to an acute sense of scholarly literary criticism—it is no accident that among the censors are many professors of English. *Titus An-*

dronicus is the curiosity among Shakespeare's works. Almost certainly, he did not write most of it, but only edited the work of some inferior author, enriching it here and there with a line or a brief passage of his own. Yet Shakespearean textual critics have by their sense of style agreed on the passages that have the Shakespearean "feel." A good mail censor must possess a similar instinct. Take for a concrete although obvious example an airmail letter dated April 15, 1941, posted at New York, addressed to a certain person at Lisbon, Portugal, signed simply "Joe," and opened at Bermuda by the British censors. Typewritten in English, its first phrase, "about a week already," put the censor on the alert. That was a German idiom. This misplacing of an adverb is an old trick of German dialect comedians. A few lines later, it occurred again, "I wrote a few times already." There were other violations of English usage such as, "It would greatly oblige as well me as him." The writer, then, was a German. That fact was not in itself damning; "Joe" might be a loyal German-American. But it suggested further search.

The British censors analyzed the contents. This was a business letter, with repeated allusions to "merchandise," "samples," "customers," and "shipments." But nowhere was there a word revealing the nature of the business— vagueness marked the whole document. The censors translated those words into terms of espionage—"facts" for merchandise, "information" for samples, "agents" for customers, "messages" for shipments—and it made sense. The letter passed on to the laboratory, where chemists applied reagents to make invisible ink visible. What emerged was writing in plain English—a compact report on the New York water front, beginning, "On April 14 was at pier 97 [Manhattan] the Norwegian *M.S. Tai Shan*—6,301 tons gray superstructure, cannon aft . . . at pier 90 the English ship *Southern Princess* 6,000 tons built like a railroad ferry steamer—two black funnels aft." And so on, with the location and appearance of every deep-sea vessel at the Manhattan docks that day and with added details concerning the morale, discipline, and habits of the crews.

This letter went back to our federal authorities and appeared some months later in court—for the author was Kurt Frederick Ludwig, to whom we have so often referred. He was in a jam. Something had happened to cut his communications, and so he took a chance with the British censor. Why he did not encipher that message in invisible ink on the back of the letter, does not appear. The address in Lisbon, was, of course, his "drop."

Not every letter leaving our shores for Europe, Africa, or South America is inspected so narrowly as was this one. However, in collaboration with the British, our censors have built up a suspect list of very many thousand persons and firms; their letters always get special attention. Not all firms or individuals so listed are suspected of espionage or known to hold sentiments that might lead to espionage; the censors watch also for people who may be trading with the enemy, defrauding the government, or trying to beat the import quotas. The main positive benefit consists in tips to our intelligence on probable spies and their methods. The negative value is even greater. The spy hesitates to take a chance with the foreign mails.

There is an even more severe watch on cablegrams and radiograms. Outgoing and incoming messages in the recognized commercial code are allowed. But try a private code or introduce cryptic phrases, and you will find yourself in trouble!

Two years before we entered the war, the F.C.C. had ordered the 100,000 radio operators of the United States to prove their citizenship and identity, and had required all short-wave stations to take and preserve recordings of their broadcasts. After Pearl Harbor, it put our 210 foreign-language stations under surveillance, and arranged a voluntary censorship among our domestic short-wave stations. Some of the rules for curbing espionage by radio puzzle the layman. Why, for example, should the F.C.C. order that stations should ignore all requests to repeat a favorite musical selection on a certain date? Because a trick like that has been employed in the past to flash a single, important fact to a concealed short-wave station in touch with the enemy.

On the very day of Pearl Harbor, our organization for radio interception went to work. Scattered through our states and our colonial possessions are ninety-one listening posts or "monitoring" stations manned by specialists, provided with direction finders, antennas, frequency-measuring equipment, and recording machines. Night and day they maintain surveillance over the whole radio spectrum. Even before we declared war, their work against the Gestapo spies had perfected their technique of locating enemy transmitters. First, two or more listening posts take the bearings of the outlaw station and chart its "lines." By noting where the lines from the intercepting stations cross, they determine its position within fifty miles or less. Into that territory go mobile stations on trucks; their crews shrink the suspected area to a radius of a city block. Operators on foot follow along with a small, highly sensitive piece of apparatus by which they spot not only the house but the very room from which the signals proceed.

Before our war was four days old, the interceptors won their first skirmish of the air. Between Pearl Harbor and the German declaration of war on us, they picked up a station monotonously repeating the letters *UA*. The two letters, instead of the usual three for a station call, aroused acute suspicion, as did the fact that there was no answer. Interceptors from coast to coast took bearings. These showed that the call came from the District of Columbia or adjacent districts in Maryland and Virginia. Twenty-four hours later—on December 10 to be exact—the mobile stations and men afoot located the transmitter in the German embassy at Washington! It is possible to determine not only where and what any enemy station is shooting, but its target as well. During the trial of the Duquesne conspirators, an expert took the stand and proved to the satisfaction of the jury that Sebold's transmitting station on Long Island was sending to a receiving station near Hamburg, Germany—the main center for German intelligence.

Acme

GEORGE JOHN DASCH, GERMAN SABOTEUR, WHOSE CONSPICUOUS APPEARANCE MADE HIS CAPTURE EASY.

Acme

EDWARD JOHN KERLING, ONE OF THE SIX GERMAN SABOTEURS EXECUTED AT WASHINGTON ON AUGUST 8, 1942.

Wide World Photos

INCENDIARY AND EXPLOSIVE DEVICES BURIED BY THIS RING OF SABOTEURS IN THE SANDS OF LONG ISLAND.

"PABLO" WABERSKI, THE
ONLY SPY SENTENCED TO
DEATH IN THE UNITED
STATES BETWEEN 1865
AND 1942 (AND HE WAS
NOT EXECUTED).

Brown Brothers

SPIES AND OPIUM SMUGGLERS OFTEN HIDE MESSAGES OR "HOP" IN
TOILET ARTICLES.

If short-wave radio is the greatest device of all for spy communication, it is also the most tricky and dangerous to the spy. The experts of the United Nations are using interception not only for counterespionage and counter-propaganda but for espionage of our own. The F.C.C. keeps a sleepless ear attuned to enemy propaganda, enemy cipher messages to and from spies, even enemy military orders. The main listening posts against Hitler and Mussolini are in London and an eastern city of the United States; against Japan, in Portland, Oregon. The listeners are not only perfect linguists—sixty tongues are represented among them—but men thoroughly acquainted with the countries over which the dictators have spread their webs; and they have advice and counsel from high psychologists, trained intelligence officers, and former foreign correspondents. As every officer who has questioned prisoners knows, even if the man whom you have on the grill lies, from his falsehoods the expert can sometimes deduce truth. This exacting, expensive work has been valuable in divining the intentions of the enemy. But its main accomplishment is also its main object—spotting spies and finding out what they are transmitting.

No activity of our secret war is so secret as this battle of the air. But on January 22, 1943, the public was allowed a momentary glimpse. Axis "drops" in South America and especially in the Argentine had been the headache of American counterespionage. A few days previously, Chile, fed up with spies, finally broke relations with the Axis countries, and the Argentine tardily forced the recall of Captain Dietrich Niebuhr, naval attaché of the German embassy, who had made Buenos Aires the spy center of the Americas. On that day, the American Advisory Committee for Political Defense of the Continent, meeting in Montevideo, published a long memorandum to vindicate its position. This included evidence against twenty-four German spies in four rings, each operating a short-wave radio station. The proof consisted mostly of intercepted messages, sent from the Argentine to Berlin, concerning the movements of merchant ships, convoys, and naval vessels— the first cause for many a tragedy of the deep—the organization of our armies, our naval tactics, our new weapons, the output of our munitions factories. And the memorandum added that our intelligence services gathered all this from its listening posts in the United States.

Some of the messages intercepted in the mails or taken with effects of arrested spies, and virtually all of the communications from the short-wave stations, are written in cipher or code or both. Unless the formula to solve them is already known, they go at once to those indispensable experts—the cryptanalysts, or cipher solvers.

These men and women are as essential to modern war as airplanes or tanks. Specialized mathematicians of high degree, they also possess creative imagination and developed intuition. We have described the ABC of cipher creation. The first principles of cipher cracking are equally simple; after which both arts soar into the empyrean of the higher arithmetic. In all written languages with a phonetic alphabet, some letters occur more often than others. In English, for example, *e* is the commonest, *z* the rarest. This is the basis of that useful manual, the frequency table. It recognizes two types of English, literary and telegraphic; the former is the one we use in our letters, newspapers, and books, the latter that condensed, cut-to-the-bone kind by which we save on telegraph tolls. The order of frequency in literary English begins:

E,T,A,O,I,N,S, etc., to Z.

The frequency table goes on to the common combinations of two letters. In literary English, their order of frequency is:

TH, EH, OH, AN, RE, HE, IN, ED, etc.

Trigraphs are three-letter combinations. The order of their frequency in literary English runs:

THE, AND, THA, ENT, ION, TIO, etc.

Then come the frequencies of double letters such as *ee* and *nn* and of two-, three-, and four-letter words such as *of, the,* and *that.* Finally, all languages have special characteristics. In English, for example, *q* is always followed by *u,* and *j* and *v* by a vowel. Of course, we have similar frequency tables for all the other phonetic languages. Not that the ciphered messages as they reach the solver's desk usually commit the gross blunder of betraying frequencies. Their intricacies guard against one invariable symbol for one letter; in a well-conceived cipher, *ss* would never be represented by such a combination as "14–14." But as the solver goes deeper into the maze, they become of great service nevertheless.

Recently, plodding professors of English have worked out tables of word frequency for each of several different kinds of spy messages, such as naval, military, and industrial. For the time comes in the cracking of most ciphers when mathematical processes are of no more use. The solver must adopt the tedious method of trial and error, and a glimpse of one word under a set of meaningless numbers may light the way to success. In World War I a new German cipher, complex for those times, was solved when a layman suggested that it might consist in orders to propagandists, and that the cryptanalysts should try such words as *report, rumor,* and *news.* To apply this method, however, the solver needs a reasonable amount of text. A single brief message like the symbols for "Destination convoy Casablanca thirty-six ships" is almost hopeless. That is one reason why when our agencies spot a spy and discover his means of communication, they watch him and play him along for a time. They are gathering material for the cryptanalysts.

Even the puzzling "book" codes, mentioned before, yield to the slow process of applied mathematics plus frequency tables, inductive and deductive reasoning and brilliant "hunches." Colonel William C. Friedman, our most famous cryptanalyst, once cracked such a message before he determined the book that served as key. The performance seems miraculous to the layman—but it happened!

Censorship is mostly unromantic drudgery. By contrast, the next most effective agency of counterespionage has the spice of danger and the pull of adventure. This is the man in the enemy's camp, the double-crosser for patriotism's sake, who works himself into a spy ring to deceive or betray it. The case of William Sebold is likely to go down as a classic of counterespionage. As we have already written, this shrewd and courageous German-American mechanic went through the German school for spies, thereby giving us illumination on the methods of our prospective enemy. He brought to this country a German code and cipher, copies of which he transmitted at once to the F.B.I. He had instructions to set up a short-wave station which was actually installed and operated by the F.B.I. in an isolated house on Long Island. He had by now identified at least fifty German spies for our intelligence forces. Other American agents, whose identity never appeared, made contact with the spies and fed them subtly false information. Daily, the busy station on Long Island carried thousands of words of sheer poison for Admiral Canaris, since inaccurate information which an intelligence department believes as gospel is many degrees worse than useless. This job, directed by the F.B.I. and cleared through the army and navy intelligence, must have been a work of art. One or two slips, and the shrewd spymasters in Berlin would have perceived that there was something wrong with the picture. But that never happened. Equally admirable was the manner in which Sebold maintained contact with our intelligence without showing his hand to his "accomplices."

When all was ready, Uncle Sam hit from the shoulder

and made a wholesale haul of spies. In the nature of the case, they could not be convicted without the testimony of Sebold. He threw off his disguise and appeared in court. His testimony was largely responsible for the pleas of guilty or convictions of the thirty-three members of the Duquesne ring. After which, Sebold withdrew into the shadows, having lived for two years in constant danger of a stab in the back on some dark night. He was not the only counterspy we planted in the enemy camp during that period.

We had in 1918 another classic of counterespionage. Mexico was in those days a gadfly on our flank. The Germans were using it as a reservoir and rest camp for spies and saboteurs. While they waited for orders, these agents passed the time in drilling, with the object of annoying us by leading border raids of Mexican bandits. "Pablo" Waberski, German naval officer, commanded the raiders and directed the traffic in military information from the United States.

Pitted against him on the other side was Dr. Paul Altendorff, an Austrian-American loyal to the land of his adoption, an agent with a touch of genius. He had served as a colonel in Carranza's Mexican Army. He spoke German, knew German psychology. Altendorff drifted across the border and, impersonating a German spy temporarily in hiding, joined Waberski's raiders, learned all that was useful to us about their plots, and proposed one of his own. Our Negroes, he said, were growing disaffected—especially the soldiers among them. He himself had already started them on the road to rebellion. With a little sympathy and encouragement, they would take the plunge. Suppose Waberski, furnished with the proper credentials, sneaked across the Rio Grande with him, met the head men of the disaffected troops on American soil and promised that if they started a Negro rebellion, Germany, when the war was won, would grant them Arkansas and Louisiana as an all-black republic?

It sounds fantastic; but Germans, as Altendorff knew, have an optimistic habit of exaggerating any differences of opinion in an enemy country. Waberski took the bait. Fish and fisherman swam the Rio Grande into the landing net of the American counterespionage. Searching Waberski, our agents found damning documents concealed in the sole of his shoe.

He was tried, found guilty, sentenced to death—the only death sentence for espionage in the United States between the Civil War and the affair of the eight saboteurs in 1942. By this time, however, insiders at Washington knew that the sands were running low for Germany. President Wilson, who must sign the death warrant before it could be executed, mercifully withheld his hand until the Armistice of November 11 ended the war. . . . Just so when the remnants of the Confederate Army, retreating to its last stand at Appomattox, caught two Union spies, the chivalrous Robert E. Lee "delayed" signing the order of execution. With so much blood spilled, why unnecessarily spill any more?

After the Armistice, Wilson commuted Waberski's sentence to imprisonment. When a few years later he became the hero of a disastrous fire in the penitentiary where he was confined, a presidential pardon freed him and he went back to Germany and to the Iron Cross— with the approval, be it said, of the American officers who convicted him. According to them, he was a brave fellow, who had only done his duty to his country as they had done theirs.

Some minor but clean-cut illustrations of such inside work during the earlier war survive in the records of our "intelligence police," the A.E.F. spyhunters. One of them, Peter De Pasqua, was Italian by origin, linguist by profession, and Red Cross interpreter at Beaune by temporary occupation. He spoke Spanish without a trace of foreign accent. His café life in Beaune brought him acquaintance and intimacy with one Diaz, a Spaniard who hated the United States because the war of 1898 had ruined his family, with another anti-American Spaniard named Ochoa, and with a Frenchman of defeatist tendencies. De Pasqua was not surprised when Diaz proposed that they four organize a ring for espionage and sabotage against the hated Yankees. De Pasqua submitted to a blood oath, put Diaz in the way of stealing some comparatively valueless plans of American works, arranged to slip past the censor letters to the German director of intelligence in Spain—probably the young naval officer who is now Admiral Canaris. De Pasqua was all set for effective work when the unexpected happened. Diaz announced a plan to blow up an American munitions dump near by; and the only way to avert a tragic disaster was to inform French counterespionage. Promptly, the

French arrested the three conspirators. However, De Pasqua had an introduction to one of Germany's directing spies. He volunteered to go to Spain and work down to the very heart of German espionage. "Do you know how likely you are to get a knife between your ribs?" asked his superior officer. "Sure!" said De Pasqua. "I'll take a chance!"

He would have gone, too, had not the Armistice ended hostilities a few days later. So the tale ends with an anticlimax, but it illustrates the methods by which a daring and ingenious agent may make himself a cog in the enemy's machine.

All Americans who crossed the Channel from France to England during the last war must remember one pleasant, minor adventure. As the alien waited at the British control for a searching inquiry as to his residence, background, credentials, and business in Britain, a well-turned-out, magnetic Englishman entered the room on some trifling errand like looking for a book or a paper and remained for light conversation on the hardships of travel in wartime, the discomforts of Continental hotels, and other trivial topics of the day.

He was the "dialect expert." He was leading the Americans to use certain English words which Germans find it difficult to pronounce. When they came out, when his keen ear caught no trace of Teutonic accent, his task was finished. And after the war ended, one of the authors learned of other subtle tricks at the control station. One of them was to put an inconspicuous symbol, like that with which a crooked gambler marks the back of a card,

on the passport of a suspect. To every military and civilian and policeman in the kingdom, it meant "look out
for this chap!"

These were only outcroppings of the third most effective method for detecting spies—shrewd agents at the
points through which they are most likely to travel, the
places where they are most likely to work. Adding the
port authorities, border guards, and local policemen to
the secret services, one realizes that by 1943 this job
probably employed more American men and women
than any other department of counterespionage.

The seaports and airports first: there we have our own
subtle methods of scrutinizing passengers from abroad,
akin to those the British employed at Folkstone or Dover,
but not now to be described. The ports: an expanded
and specially trained coast guard watches the approaches
to wharves and warehouses, marks and follows suspicious
characters. The coastline: that same force, put on its
mettle by the affair of the eight saboteurs, has its eye
on every furlong. The land borders: patrols far more
complete and spywise than their predecessors of 1917
keep them under equally close observation.

"Where spies are most likely to work"—that includes
a world in itself. Obviously, spies and flies gather about
a naval station or a military camp; we must take sanitary
precautions against both. We do. "The last people you
would suspect" watch in the surrounding cafés, night
clubs, soda fountains, and honky-tonks not only for persons who show undue interest in naval and military affairs
but also for loose-tongued sailors and soldiers, civilian

employees of military posts, and munitions workers. Washington is highly important in this respect. A spy turned loose in certain files would be in paradise. Hence the precautions which so irritate the unthinking visitor to some offices—preliminary correspondence, letters of identification, permits, badges bearing the wearer's photograph. Even the employees must wear those badges. . . . It is said that a government clerk with a reckless sense of humor once replaced the photograph on his badge with a bijou portrait of Adolf Hitler and wore it for three weeks before the guards noticed it. In spite of this one comic incident, these precautions make life more precarious and operations more difficult for spies. . . . The visitor to important offices in the Pentagon —the army's new, labyrinthine office building—is met by a guard who sticks to him like a shadow until he leaves. At that, there are still potential leaks in Washington, for we are careless people. Said an officer of military intelligence: "It seems to me that I never go home in a streetcar but I look over the shoulder of some passenger and see that he is reading a document or paper marked 'confidential.' " . . . These precautions do not mark Washington alone; they prevail wherever there is real need for secrecy. Those important munitions plants wherein the army and navy co-operate with the management are even more strictly watched and guarded.

No man or woman enters government service even as a munitions worker until government agents or the personnel department of his factory have looked into his past, even to his ancestry. Men and women with enemy aliens for parents are not barred per se; but the burden of proving loyalty lies on them. The fingerprints of every applicant go to the F.B.I. for comparison with the sixty million prints in their classified files. That precaution sometimes gets real results, as when one elderly man's prints came back with the report, "Arrested for espionage, 1917." The files have shown that others have criminal records. Although an individual in this class may have led an upright life for years, Uncle Sam usually takes no chances with a relapse. Even after the employee enters the service, government agents watch men whose positions give them access to secret files or knowledge of hidden intentions toward the enemy—watch them especially to see whether they are yielding to the human weakness for making oneself interesting by spilling "inside stuff." European intelligence often puts agents even on responsible statesmen or high-ranking officers. We might do the same, with occasional profit!

Now and then the newspapers carry brief notices to the effect that just so many dangerous enemy aliens, the names usually withheld, have been interned by orders of the Attorney General. Behind most of these internments there is the story of a long, careful operation, sometimes solely by the F.B.I., sometimes in collaboration with army and navy intelligence and the local police— who in most cities are giving cheerful and intelligent help. Although it would be impracticable to furnish the police, European-fashion, with a pedigree of each arriving guest, the hotels are not overlooked—especially the largest and most famous of them and certain more obscure ones which for various reasons spies might use. Since soldiers, sailors, and marines are traveling everywhere, the hot spots in interior towns are nearly as important as those in the region of seaports and camps. Experience proves that the hotter and more disreputable the spot, the more likely it is to be a haunt of spies. An old European character has appeared here—the pimp whose white slaves make him a double income by practicing two professions, prostitution and espionage.

Persons surreptitiously heiling Hitler in our German districts or whispering *vivas* to Mussolini in our Little Italies may be the best friends of our democracy. We have mentioned that Ellis Island case in which a band of Germans, rounded up for deportation, even in the detention pen tried to recruit spies and fifth columnists for Hitler. Among these "arrested" persons were government agents, playing the old game; we are still making use of facts which they gathered during that operation.

Among our aliens of enemy extraction there are borderline cases. What, exactly, shall we do with a German woman who wants Hitler to win and says so in private, but who has never joined a seditious organization, tried to subvert our soldiers nor given aid and comfort to the enemy? With an adolescent nourished in Nazi propaganda, who is foolishly shooting off his mouth? With a grown man who has been seen behaving strangely and in strange company but whom our spyhunters have never caught in any overt act? The enemy-alien boards sitting as half-official courts all over the country exist to deal with such problems as that. They weigh the evidence, which includes anonymous tips from private citizens—mostly true and sincere in motive but sometimes imaginative and malicious—and dispose of the case. Some of the accused might be dangerous; they go into detention for the duration. Others are put on parole; still others kept under close surveillance. Typically, the members of these boards are highly intelligent men and women; and the system has worked.

Much evidence against suspects in this class and, indeed, against actual spies comes from the local police. All law-enforcement officers have to adjust their mental attitudes and working methods before they can succeed in the work of counterespionage. In peace, the police exist solely to guard us against violators of law and order. Criminals, delinquents, and misdemeanants as a class are people of low intelligence. Aside from the small mercenaries, spies are at least as intelligent as the police who pursue them. And some of the keenest brains in the world direct their operations. More importantly, the objects of police work against criminals and counterespionage work against spies are fundamentally different.

The police detective assigned to solve a crime and bring the criminal to justice proceeds on comparatively straight lines. He looks into the case until he finds reason to suspect an individual. He arrests the suspect, gathers enough evidence to warrant indictment and promise conviction—and that is all until the day in court. Arrest them, convict them—that principle is ground into every civilian policeman. The expert spyhunter, on the other hand, sails a course as devious as that of a destroyer dodging bombs and torpedoes at the same time. He is interested in convictions as a deterrent measure. But his two primary objects, one just as important as the other, are to keep his adversary from gathering information and to make such information as the enemy does receive so inaccurate as to be worse than useless.

Arresting a small spy like the bartender in a waterfront saloon is a comparatively futile proceeding. This man, even if he breaks down and confesses, can usually name only the associate who brings him his pay and carries away his information. It is far better to watch him until you identify his link with the rest of the spy chain and work up link by link to the brains of the operation, who knows all. Along the way, the expert spyhunter uncovers the pattern of the operation, including "drops," codes, and all other means of communication. So far this does not much differ from the technique of Thomas A. Dewey when he smashed the gangs of commercial racketeers in New York.

Having gone thus far, however, expert counterspies do not, like Dewey, invariably scoop up the gang. A major objection to arresting a ring is the fact that as soon as their silence warns the enemy, he sends in another set to cover the same ground—and the spyhunter must begin all over again. And a set of industrious but unsuspecting spies may be turned into a weapon against your enemy. Sometimes the counterspies insinuate into the ring one or more agents who feed its members false or misleading information. Sometimes they secretly arrest the whole lot and, with the aid of those expert, non-criminal forgers whom they can always command, send false but convincing information straight to the enemy's departments of intelligence. Sometimes, indeed, they find an individual or a small group so inept that it is best to let them alone. The authors could name one or two individuals who worked straight through World War I as spies for the Central Powers, were perfectly known as such to the French or British, and never had a hand laid on them. Free, they boggled a job that better spies would have done well; further, they furnished glimpses of the enemy's intentions and methods.

Counterspies following spies; counter-counter-spies following counterspies—it becomes as complex as an Einstein formula.

> Big fleas have little fleas
> Upon their backs to bite 'em.
> And little fleas have lesser fleas—
> So on, ad infinitum.

The following is an instance of counter-counter-espionage which, unfortunately, the authors cannot in decency tell with all the names, dates, and places. But it happened.

Cappadocia, let us say, was at war with Germany; the United States was not—as yet. The doorkeeper of the Cappadocian ministry at Washington was a retired non-commissioned officer with a chestful of medals. A set of German counterspies wooed him with beer; and he was shrewd enough to estimate them for what they were and lead them on. When they had established his disloyalty to

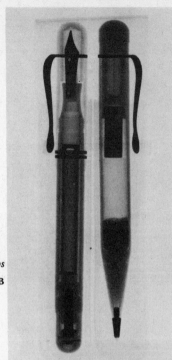

Wide World Photos

A MODERN INCENDIARY TIME BOMB
DISGUISED AS A FOUNTAIN PEN.

Brown Brothers

WRECKAGE OF THE BLACK TOM EXPLOSION IN NEW YORK HARBOR,
1916. THIS WAS THE BIGGEST SINGLE SABOTAGE OPERATION IN
HISTORY.

Official U.S. Navy Photograph

PHOTOGRAPHIC INTELLIGENCE. AERIAL VIEW OF LUNGA AIRPORT,
WHICH THE JAPANESE BUILT ON GUADALCANAL ISLAND.

Official U.S. Navy Photograph

LIEUTENANT COMMANDER PETER C. HOLM, U.S.N., QUESTIONS A
JAPANESE PRISONER TAKEN IN THE ALEUTIANS.

their own satisfaction, they made their proposition. They could pay five hundred dollars for the whole pattern, the blueprint, as it were, of Cappadocian intelligence in the United States. . . . A characteristic German proceeding this. They cannot conceive of an improvised operation. Everything must be thought out, organized in advance, and, even though a secret, diagramed on paper. . . . The doorman responded that he would see what he could do. Meantime, he was reporting constantly to the Cappadocian Chief of Intelligence in the United States. The chief accommodated the Germans with an imaginative but convincing document. He was about to send it to the doorman when he had an inspiration. In this country lived hundreds of Cappadocians of military age who had refused to go home and enlist. The chief, chuckling to himself, typed out their names and addresses, headed the list, "Cappadocian spies in the United States," and sent it along with the "pattern" of Cappadocian intelligence. A few days, and the slackers were running to the Cappadocian ministry and consulates to complain that they were being followed on the streets, that mysterious thieves had stolen confidential documents from their office files, that people looked over their transoms at night. Some of them grew so nervous that they went home and enlisted as the lesser of two evils.

Only the limits of human ingenuity bind the subtle tricksters of this curious trade. For example:

In August, 1914, while the German Army was still driving on toward Paris, the British arrested Karl Hans Lody, an officer of German military intelligence, who had entered England on a purloined American passport. With considerable publicity, they shot him in the Tower of London. Thereafter, whenever they spotted a German spy the British did not arrest him until they had learned his instructions, had established his method of communication and found his code or cipher. Then they laid hands on him and shot him. Next day, a three-line item on the front page of every British newspaper announced that a spy designated as X-22 or by a similar meaningless set of letters and figures had been executed the day before—no more than that. After which, they continued to send plausible but doctored information in his hand and cipher and through his regular "drop." When this had happened six or seven times, the Germans paused and took stock. They had been working in England on the British method—single, highly expert spies, unknown to each other. All of these people were reporting regularly; yet seven or eight had been shot. Ergo, some of the messages were faked. But which ones? This quandary cast doubt on all information received from England, forced them to wipe the slate clean and to begin all over again.

The reader must have noticed that when a spy goes to jail or to trial, the F.B.I. always stands as the body responsible for the arrest and that its agents are usually the chief witnesses. He may have inferred from this circumstance that it is the sole agency for counterespionage in the United States. It is not, of course, for there are military and naval intelligence and certain other agencies. The first tip on the most vital evidence on a spy

or a spy ring may come from any one of them, but the
F.B.I. serves as the co-ordinating agency. Night and day,
the F.B.I. maintains close contact with other agencies.

The fourth important agency of counterespionage is
the private citizen neither in uniform nor in government
service. His main usefulness is negative—keeping his
mouth shut and encouraging others to do the same. In
another chapter, we shall deal more fully with that function and with other ways in which he may help. When
a private citizen brings information on a suspected person, our authorities discourage all spyhunting after his
initial tip; otherwise he may drop a monkey wrench into
a most delicate piece of machinery. Still, occasionally the
novice does a brilliant piece of work on his own. As witness the Swiss consulate case in World War I.

On February 1, 1917, the United States broke relations with Germany. For some unknown reason, the
German diplomats here decided not to destroy their
papers, documents, and archives. The Swiss served as
German chargés d'affaires; as neutrals, their premises
were immune from search. So the Germans wrapped up
their papers in neat parcels, packed them into locked
and sealed cases and stored them in the Swiss consulate
at New York. Our government wanted to look at those
papers. But that seemed impossible.

It did not seem so impossible to a pair of brothers
listed in the Social Register and the Directory of Directors, and but lately enlisted as agents of the F.B.I. In
that period, that force was less highly organized than it
is today. Carefully omitting to notify Bruce Bielaski, the

brothers went on a hunt of their own. When they rented a suite in the same building with the Swiss consulate, they asked if they might use their offices of nights for a quiet game of poker with friends. The agent for the building was glad to do this little favor for men so prominent in society, so powerful in finance. The game went on night after night. Occasionally, two or three of the players dropped out for a few hands and strolled into the hall. They were observing the habits of the watchman. When they had the pattern of his movements, a new acquaintance of theirs, a man not listed in the Social Register, and far too expert with keys, entered the consulate, unlocked the cases, revealed the German documents. On subsequent nights, deserters from the poker game opened the neat parcels, took the documents, replaced them with old newspapers cut to appropriate size, resealed and repacked them so that they seemed undisturbed. Then they moved the loot—two truckloads of it—to an empty house and slipped to Bielaski an anonymous message informing him that if he would send his minions to such and such an address, he would find documents most useful to prosecution of the war. Mr. Bielaski is not a man who needs a second hint. He promptly collected the papers—which included all the records of the German secret service in this country from 1914 until February 1, 1917. But had the Swiss Government found out about this operation, Bielaski could truthfully have sworn in court that he had no knowledge or information concerning the persons who had so shockingly violated international etiquette!

British intelligence has always noted with grim amusement that the German spy cannot resist a besetting temptation to make written notes on matters that should be recorded only in the human memory. There was much gold in this pile; and also one diamond as big as the Kohinoor—a list, with addresses, of every person who was serving or who had served here as a German spy or saboteur between 1914 and 1917. The F.B.I. was able at once to lay its hands on men whom no one had ever before suspected of hostile or treasonable intentions.

Continental European espionage has always proceeded on the theory that the national interest sweetens all crimes and offenses against common morals, from murder on down the list. However, it has remained for the Gestapo to introduce kidnaping as a method of counterespionage. Even before the attack on Poland, they were crossing the border of little, impotent Switzerland, grabbing Jewish or liberal refugees who knew too much about the Nazi party and carrying them back to Germany to be liquidated. One or two cases of this kind got into the newspapers; and many intelligence officers believe these tactics of the Gestapo account for the fate of certain refugees who got as far as Switzerland and then disappeared. Once at least the revolutionary underground in Germany has imitated the methods of its enemy, minus the liquidation at the end. One of their members was losing his nerve; also, the Gestapo had spotted him. If he was arrested, he would probably tell everything. He wanted to get away to Switzerland, but could not summon enough courage to make the attempt. Whereupon, his comrades kidnaped him, carried him to the border, slipped through a hole they had found in the police cordon, and released him on neutral soil.

In November, 1939, Germany was at war with Poland, France, and Britain, but the Netherlands were still neutral. Early in the war—if you believe Berlin—the Gestapo counterspies had slipped one over on British intelligence. A set of agents professing to be socialists in revolt against Nazi rule had volunteered as British spies, gratefully received a short-wave radio transmitter, and gone back to Germany, from which they sent doctored information. On the eighth of November, someone planted a bomb in the ceiling of the Munich beer hall where Hitler was speaking. Unfortunately, the Führer for once made a short speech and had left the hall before it exploded.

Next day—still according to the Germans—a decoy message from that supposedly secret and friendly spy ring lured Captain Richard Henry Stevens and Sigismund Payne Best, British intelligence agents, to the Netherlands border town of Venloo. The rest is certain. As they arrived at the frontier in their car, a squad of Gestapo agents in civilian dress rushed across the line onto Netherlands soil, drove Dutch civilians away by a fusillade of pistol shots, murdered the chauffeur, seized the British agents, handcuffed them, carried them away to Berlin, accused them of framing the plot to murder Hitler.

It was one of those heavy, dramatic coups that Germans love. It gave, of course, great prestige to the Gestapo and a jarring blow to British intelligence, which had

scored so often against them in the past. But the operation had its more practical uses. These were trained veterans; some consider Stevens one of the best operatives
the British had. They knew a good deal about British
secret service. Under scientific questioning, they might
reveal much of it. And if questioning failed, there remained physical torture—a method the Nazis do not
hesitate to use. In that, as in all things else, they have
gone back to the Dark Ages.

CHAPTER SIX

THE FURTIVE WEAPON:
SABOTAGE

WHEN it comes to sabotage, we must define terms.

Destruction of the enemy arms and supplies by soldiers in uniform is a piece of tactics as old as warfare. To take a famous example from American history: In 1862 Jeb Stuart led a daring cavalry raid around McClellan's army before Richmond, in the course of which he burned or blew up several million dollars' worth of Union munitions, ammunition, and provisions. The devastating air raids on such centers of war industry as Coventry, Turin, and Cologne are the modern equivalent. If at times civilian agents in enemy territory damaged lines of communication or ruined supplies, these were until 1914 sporadic acts. No one thought of organizing the process until World War I taught soldiers slowly and painfully that while armies trod the road to victory, industry built the roadbed; that munitions were as vital and necessary as men. The Germans, as usual, were the first to learn and apply the lesson. On the one hand, they began to organize their war industries on an all-out scale. On the other, realizing that the United States was the "arsenal of democracy," they sent or recruited agents to hamper our production of munitions by fomenting labor disturbances, damaging factories, destroying finished products, concealing time bombs in ships carrying munitions to Allied Europe. If these tactics were not sufficient to have much effect on the course of the war, it was because the Germans were still only feeling their way and employed some very inept agents. Later in the same war, the subject and rebellious peoples of the Central Empires like the Czechs in Austria-Hungary and the Poles in German Poland themselves began to blow up munitions factories, derail trains, send supplies awry, and put sand in gears. But these operations were small, sporadic, and often organized only in the most rudimentary way.

In the labor struggles of the nineteenth century, radical French unionists, prevented for one reason or another from striking, used to slow down production by damaging machinery. Dropping their wooden shoes or *sabots* into the wheels, looms, or gears was a standard trick. Hence the name "sabotage." Strictly interpreted, it means the secret process of hampering production of munitions or destroying them by means of agents or sympathizers in civilian dress. When a British force raids the Continental coast and blows up a munitions dump, when an airplane drops bombs on a factory, or when a submarine sinks a ship loaded with airplane engines, that is not sabotage; it is only an old, recognized form of military tactics.

For some new devices of totalitarian warfare we still have no satisfactory names. When we speak of "psychological sabotage" we are using a figure of speech for want of a more concrete term. It refers, of course, to the process of breaking down the resistance of an army or a population by treason, by agents who spread dire rumors and reports, and by mendacious broadcasts and literature. These proceedings belong really to the field of propaganda, which we have felt obliged generally to ignore in this book. Nevertheless physical sabotage often works so closely with psychological sabotage that it cannot entirely be overlooked.

When after the peace of Versailles such wide-thinking German soldiers as Colonel Walther Nicolai began laying plans for a new era of conquest, they noted sabotage and propaganda as means to victory with which Germany had merely trifled in World War I but henceforth should exploit to the limits of their possibilities. General Karl Haushofer called attention to the supreme importance of the enemy's "industrial anatomy." This, rather than the army or navy, he wrote, should be the prime object of attack. Hitler echoed these sentiments in *Mein Kampf;* and the Nazi regime was scarcely established before he had founded a school for saboteurs which is still in operation. The basic training in this establishment does not much differ from that in the school for spies—methods for crossing borders, shadowing and avoiding shadows, wireless telegraphy, cipher writing, and the like. Then the student saboteur branches away from the embryo spies and finishes his education with special courses that include the use of explosive and thermite incendiary bombs, methods for crippling machinery, for checking the flow of a continuous process, for damaging enemy reservoirs, oil storage tanks, wharves, and electric power plants.

Hitler's sensational Polish campaign served as a rehearsal for the blitzkrieg that in less than three months overwhelmed Norway, the Netherlands, Denmark, Belgium, and France. On its purely military side, this was a daring tactical co-ordination with ground forces of all the elements in mechanized warfare, including tanks, bombing planes and fighting planes with unheard-of power and speed. But as all the world now knows, his long psychological preparation by means of secret agents and fifth columnists was just as much a part of his strategic plan as his mechanized army. When the hour of action neared, a skirmish line of saboteurs preceded the army. Some were Germans long established in the territory of his prospective enemies, some members of the fascist groups built up by his propagandists and often financed from Berlin, some new arrivals who in civilian clothes or in uniforms of the hostile army dropped from the clouds in parachutes. Not until World War II is over will the historians of this time find it possible to sift truth from rumor and reconstruct the full pattern of these operations. But already we know its outlines. Into armies confused by the bewildering speed of German operations and hampered by a flood of civilian refugees came German agents uniformed as high officers of their own armies who by personal commands or forged papers ordered whole divisions to retreat or to move to points where they were as useless as a troop of Boy Scouts. Secret radio stations broadcast rumors that generated panic. Headquarters ordered troops to blow up important bridges and they were not blown up—we may never know exactly why.

These tricks of omission and commission—and a thousand more of the same kind—constituted "psychological sabotage." The physical saboteurs were even more busy. Bridges which French divisions must cross if they would get into action were dynamited in spite of guards that seemed strong enough for the purpose. Just before the German army attacked a Dutch town, squads of men in peasant clothes would emerge from barges that had come through the canals and docked a day or two before, proceed to telephone and radio stations and power plants, draw weapons from under their smocks, and either take possession or put dynamos and wires out of commission. Munitions dumps went up in single cosmic explosions and reserve gasoline tanks in torrents of flame, troop trains plunged over embankments, airplanes rose only to flutter down to disastrous crash. These are only samples —a mere catalogue of the various devices for paralyzing resistance to the blitzkrieg would fill many pages.

But the point is that the Germans had incorporated sabotage into the tactical scheme of modern war. In the first major campaign it succeeded even beyond their expectations. It did not work quite so well in the Yugoslavian and Greek campaigns, partly because the Italians, who fought the first battles, applied fifth-column tactics less expertly than their masters, partly because by the time the Germans arrived to give the *coup de grace,* the

Greeks and the loyal elements of Yugoslavia were fore-warned. Finally when Hitler came to attack Russia it did not work at all. As stated before, when the Russians satisfied themselves that a German invasion was only a matter of days, they rounded up the fifth column, the spies and the saboteurs, already catalogued by the efficient N.K.V.D., and shot them to the last man. The first campaign of the Russo-German War was a blitzkrieg without benefit of psychological warfare or sabotage. Hitler had played out his hand.

Or rather, the play had passed to his enemies. They had learned the game of sabotage, both physical and mental, and were trumping the aces of its inventor. Russia did not exactly take the lead on the Allied side, but while we are on the subject, let us finish with her operations. "Leading them on" has always been a principle of Russian strategy against an invader; and we have the word of Ambassador Joseph E. Davies for the fact that Russians are the greatest saboteurs in the world. When they saw that an attack by Germany was inevitable, Stalin and his advisers conceived an original and daring plan. As usual the army would make a fighting retreat. But it would leave behind it civilian sabotage groups to wage an integrated war on the enemy's lines of communication. When these were stretched too far and had begun to snap under a double strain, the army would counterattack. However, the Russians had overestimated their ability to slow up a blitzkrieg. The Germans advanced so rapidly that the distance between the army and the saboteur groups became too great for efficient co-operation and the initial plan, while it had a few tactical successes, failed as a whole.

Whereupon the Russian General Staff shifted to Plan Two. They maintained the sabotage groups but gave them more or less liberty of action. And they added guerilla bands composed of expert shots and daring raiders. The main object was to hamper enemy transportation, destroy enemy material; if, incidentally, they destroyed a few enemy soldiers, so much the better. All during the first German advance, they blew up munitions dumps, derailed trains, set fire to storehouses of provisions and winter clothes and to gasoline tanks, hampered, irritated, and delayed the enemy by a thousand subtle tricks. As the German drive slowed up because of the distances it had traversed, they established—largely by radio and plane—better liaison with the Supreme Command. And the General Staff has given them credit for one victory in the field. In the autumn of 1941, having taken the Crimea, the Germans advanced on Rostov, gateway to the Caucasus. The panzer elements dashed on and took the city. But they had outrun their supply columns. Thereupon—and by preconceived plan—the saboteurs and guerillas closed in on the lines of supply, paying special attention to oil and gasoline. The tanks and mechanized divisions established at Rostov found themselves literally out of gas. Spies reported this; and Timoshenko's divisions swept down from the hills surrounding the city, drove the Germans out and captured their immobilized tanks and mechanical transport. When in the spring of 1942 the Germans started their drive into the Caucasus, they had to take Rostov again; and the delay may have saved the Grozny and Baku oil fields.

By the spring of 1942, when Germany opened the second all-out drive against Russia, the Soviet Government had perfected its loose but effective system of sabotage behind the enemy lines. When the Germans occupied a town, the head men among the inhabitants dug up buried rifles and machine guns, got away to some rendezvous in a forest or gorge, joined or organized a guerilla band, and made sudden forays on oil tanks, railroads, and supply dumps. The other inhabitants, living in squalor and misery and on the verge of starvation, were their accomplices and turned many a trick on their own account. The Germans took stern measures to enforce the old rule of war that they themselves first laid down —that an ununiformed civilian who raises his hand against an army of invasion must die the death of a spy. The newsreels and illustrated weeklies have shown us German photographs of poor frozen corpses hanging in Russian villages as a warning to the inhabitants. These were mostly saboteurs. Never, it would seem, could the Germans spare enough troops from front-line operations to guard perfectly their long line of communication. These saboteurs have outweighed many a division in their value to the Russian cause.

When the Nazis swept up western Europe, the governments were as ill prepared in the matter of sabotage as in every other respect. The underground sprang from the hearts of the people. Little groups of valiant patriots, burning with the shame of their easy defeat and with loathing for their conquerors, began to unite for resistance. Before the Nazis perfected the guards on frontiers and seacoasts, the underground busied itself mostly with getting young men or loyal politicians out of the country in order that they might join the anti-German forces assembling in London. Then, as the war settled down to its pace, they began to amalgamate group with group and to prepare for effective internal resistance. Now, the governments-in-exile in London or Cairo had oriented themselves. By various means, but especially by radio and by agents dropped by parachutes from airplanes or smuggled across by submarine, they kept touch with their underground organizations in the homeland.

The development of the parachute jump from airplanes has given tremendous help to sabotage, for it not only enables a belligerent to drop at chosen objectives not only daring saboteurs but also explosives.

Leadership of the larger underground groups is organized like a sound spy ring. The members know as few of their associates as possible. The couriers, who carry orders and plans from headquarters, employ tricky devices to deliver their messages. For example, courier and receiver go to a Nazi-inspired meeting. As the audience strolls away, the courier talks to many people, including the man for whom his message is intended. The leaders find some plausible excuse, like a small and intimate chess club or a legitimate business, for meeting regularly. They take far greater risks than the average military spy; one slip and they are dead men. Yet millions of

Europeans are accepting that risk, soberly but gladly. "We're the condemned," one of them has said. "We're living on borrowed time. Well, everyone must die eventually!" The death toll has been high. Yet when one of the members dies on the scaffold, with his back to a wall, or in the torture chamber of a concentration camp, ten volunteers spring up to take his place.

Some of the national groups engaged in this silent struggle stand responsible to a single general headquarters situated in London, New York, or Cairo; some have two or three groups. To all these, however, we must add the communists who generally play a lone hand and are often at odds with the bourgeois groups. But all use their agents for four definite purposes.

First, keeping up national morale until the day of action. To this end work the underground publications— at present about fifteen hundred of them from real newspapers having considerable circulation down to weekly chain letters. Of course there is little truth in the Axis radio or newspapers. The British and American short-wave stations are giving them the real news—always a bit editorialized, it is true, but to the Axis-controlled radio as light is to darkness. However, listening to the radio of the "Jewish plutocracies" is a crime in Axis-controlled territories, and the truth would reach few of the captives but for the underground newspapers and especially that chain-letter plan. A head man who has taken down the London or New York broadcast from a receiver hidden in a cellar, an outhouse, or a haystack mails or passes ten copies of his transcript to trusted friends and requests them all to pass it on by the same system. Also, they pass on tiny, light-weight paper leaflets dropped by airplanes or larger ones—smuggled in—prepared by our Office of War Information. These O.W.I. messages have been reproduced in many clandestine newspapers.

The second purpose of the underground is to build the skeleton of a guerilla army against the day when the United Nations will invade Europe. When the time comes, every patriot will know his place and rank. This task is easier in territories having large areas of wild mountain land, like the Balkan countries, than in thickly settled industrial regions like Belgium and Bohemia. In Yugoslavia, as all the world knows, the guerillas are already fighting. In Greece, the nucleus for an army of liberation is hiding in the mountains. In the rest, the underground has already accumulated and hidden stores of munitions. Probably they are not enough for the purpose of arming a population, but already the United Nations are supplementing them by supplies flown in by planes or delivered by submarines. More will be sent when the day of liberation comes.

The third purpose of the underground is plain espionage. The patriot-spy in territory held by the Gestapo works under an especially acute subconscious strain. But there is one compensation: 90 per cent of the people who surround him are friends, not enemies, and will help him to get information.

The fourth purpose, for the present the main one, is physical sabotage. Ever since the Nazis began to force subject peoples into the munitions factories, this has been going on with increasing speed. Headquarters at London or Cairo determine the strategy; local leaders command or suggest the tactics. The most generally effective method is what we call "the slow down" and the British, "ca' canny." The employees move as slowly as possible; they invent ways for delaying and hampering the work of others. "Take your time when you go to the toilet," says one set of instructions. "Take drugs to give the appearance of illness, if possible get a hand or foot injured in such a manner that it will not disable you permanently. Remember your comrades at the front are suffering worse injuries for the common cause." These tactics are almost impossible to meet squarely. The Germans tried to speed up by offering bonuses for fast work; the result, fast workers found themselves ostracized. They tried punishment; the result, still slower work. Fifteen minutes a day lost by ten million workers means the loss of rifles, tanks, and airplanes by the tens of thousands.

When it comes to the actual destruction of material, the tricks are as innumerable as the devices of industry. A large-caliber cannon has a lining of specially hardened steel that wears out after some three hundred rounds of firing, whereupon the piece must be relined. Smuggle certain chemicals into the molten steel and the lining will stand up perfectly on the proving ground, but will go to pieces after about twenty-five rounds at the front. When the Germans discovered this and hunted down the stores of destructive chemicals, the workmen discovered in turn that a cup of hot tea or coffee poured down the barrel at the appropriate stage of manufacture would produce much the same effect. A pinch of the appropriate chemical in the detonator of a bomb makes it incapable of exploding; duds rendered harmless by this little piece of chicanery have dropped on England. Since Germany is hard put for a supply of gasoline, United Nations strategy has paid special attention to this prime necessity of modern war. One device is to pour into tanks or tank cars a colorless substance that does not make its presence felt until the gasoline heats up in the tank of an airplane. Then it lays down a gummy deposit that stops the works almost immediately and sends the machine to the repair shop. Every storage tank in one great consignment of gasoline bound for the front was so treated; the Germans had to send it back for refining. And so on.

Weekly, perhaps almost daily, munitions factories in occupied territory have a fire or an explosion—the work of cleverly placed thermite bombs. At the date of writing the Germans have closed most sources of news from Czechoslovakia. But they do send out the German newspapers published in Prague or Brno. And Czechs in this country have scanned with grief mingled with melancholy triumph the "execution column." "Six men [names given] hanged on conviction of taking part in the disaster to such-and-such munitions factory." "Three men shot for damaging machinery." "Seven hanged as accomplices of the traitor who burned down the Blank steel works." The dour, resolute Czechs with three hundred years of experience in resisting oppression are carrying on in spite of formal and informal executions and mass deportations that are steadily reducing the native population of Bohemia and Moravia.

Railroad transportation is another weak point in the German war economy. Tracks and rolling stock have begun to degenerate. One cause is systematic sabotage. In spite of innumerable guards, rails are loosened, switches spiked, semaphore apparatus so damaged that it fails to work at the proper time. The result is a premeditated wreck—often of a troop train or a consignment of perishable military supplies that burn up in the subsequent fires. Ammunition trains have blown up while running full speed because of delayed-action incendiary bombs planted under the wooden floors of the cars, locomotives because of a stick of capped dynamite artistically concealed in a lump of coal. Once on a line leading into Russia, such things happened so commonly that the Germans set thousands of enslaved inhabitants on the line as guards and inspectors. If any wreck happened, so many of them would be shot. Things did happen, and the Germans carried out their threat. But the sabotage continued with accelerated pace. The guards and inspectors had welcomed this chance to get at the line and offer their lives for their country. When, late in 1942, the Russians began their great counterattack and the tide turned in favor of the Allies, the Allied strategists of sabotage seem to have ordered special attention to the railroads, and the French and Norwegians took to the direct method of blowing up tracks and bridges. The wrecks on European railroads during this war have far outmatched the record of American lines in the old

days when railroading was new and safety devices unknown.

The more you run a freight car, the faster it wears out.
So, like the saboteurs of American ammunition destined
for Russia in World War I, the patriots often mislabel
the boxes containing small-arms ammunition or small-
caliber shells. When they arrive and it is perceived that
they do not fit the guns, there is more work for the railroads.

The Germans have been stripping enslaved countries
of their crops. In spite of inspectors and heavy legal
penalties, the peasants have been holding out much
produce. Farmers in Czechoslovakia were supposed to
turn in all the eggs from their hens. The Germans had
an orgy of statistics and discovered that Czech hens
seemed to be laying only 60 per cent as many eggs as hens
in Germany. Ergo—sabotage, of course. They had veter-
inarians survey the poultry yards. Nothing wrong with
the reproductive apparatus of the hens. So the Gestapo ordained drastic penalties running up to death for farmers
who ate their own eggs, and sent agents to look for damning evidence such as yolk marks on carelessly washed
pots and pans. The farmers and their families countered
by eating their eggs raw in the henhouse, burning the
shells and burying the ashes. All over occupied middle
Europe, farmers light their houses with kerosene lamps.
The conquerors allotted them small quantities of kerosene for this purpose. But the houses went dark; that
substance was too useful for tainting sacks of flour. Whole
trainloads, polluted in this manner, arrived at the front

before anyone discovered the trick. Of late, consignments of "flour," which upon being opened turned out
to be miscellaneous rubbish, have arrived in Berlin. Railroad saboteurs, collaborating with the farmers, have constantly misconsigned carloads of perishable fruits and
vegetables so that they are uneatable when the consignee
in Germany receives them.

Political assassination is a different story. The German reprisals on innocent hostages are so barbarous that
the governments-in-exile have often begged their enslaved countrymen not to kill Germans—for the present.
Often, probably, the motive for these affairs is revenge
for some intolerable outrage. Then, too, the communist
groups are playing their own game; and when the German radio announcers ascribe the assassination of some
high officer to "communist terrorists" they may come
much nearer to the truth than usual.

Sabotage—and assassination for that matter—has a
military use as potent as damage to the enemy's supplies
and disruption of his communications. It bites into manpower. Guarding against it requires whole army corps.
In the late winter of 1942–43, when the German Army
was facing disaster on the Eastern front, the High Command had to detach several divisions from the reserve
and then organize a new police force in order to deal
with the outbreak of sabotage in all the occupied countries. And both sabotage and political assassination are
effective tactics in the war of nerves.

Bringing the subject nearer home, physical sabotage in
the United States during this war reminds one of Artemus

Ward's lecture entitled "The Snakes of Ireland" which began: "My friends, there are no snakes in Ireland." We have had isolated cases of mischief to military goods in process of manufacture; but according to the F.B.I. not a single case can with certainty be traced back to the German, Italian, or Japanese war machines. From January 1, 1940, to February 1, 1943, the F.B.I. reviewed 7,400 reports of sabotage. Of these, 6,842 were false alarms or natural accidents. Of the 558 cases of real sabotage—for which up to February 1, 1943, 424 convictions had been obtained and 134 cases awaited trial—only a handful of the accused were Axis sympathizers, and they were working on their own. At the date of writing, this remains a chief mystery of World War II.

Certainly sabotage of American factories was integral to the plans of the German General Staff. As long ago as 1924, Walther Nicolai raved in print over the ineptitude of the German saboteurs who worked among us in 1915 and 1916. When he and his associates founded or revived their school of saboteurs, they had an American section whose students had lived in the United States and knew something of our industrial methods. In secret meetings, the Bund used to gloat over the destruction it would visit on our industrial machine when "the Day" struck. Going further, it worked many agents into our munitions factories. Fritz Duquesne, the German spy, in his conversations with William Sebold, our secret agent, discussed explosive and incendiary bombs and the methods he intended to employ in planting them. And other signs pointed to the same conclusion.

In the Philippines sabotage by Japanese or pro-Japanese Filipinos scored one major and one minor coup. It so crippled the aircraft-warning system that American airfields had no notice of the coming of the Japanese bombers that at one stroke deprived us of our air power, with disastrous results; and it hampered our motor torpedo boats by putting wax in their gasoline tanks.

But in the continental United States nothing happened—at least nothing that can be proved. The burning of the gigantic *Normandie-Lafayette* at her dock while in process of refitting as a transport looked at first like sabotage. Investigation showed that it was only a case of incredible carelessness on the part of a human machine not yet tuned up. The big explosion of a smokeless powder plant in New Jersey has no odor of being an enemy job. And these two are the only major disasters in our munitions industries since we began to rearm. Yet many disasters, major and minor, destroy all circumstantial evidence as to their origin. The new German "incendiary pencils," designed to generate a heat of three thousand degrees, have a shell made from material that vanishes as gas in such heat as that; and when an airplane falls, the wreck is so complete that the cause of its failure to function is often indeterminable. Constantly we read of bombers or transport planes that crash in the process of training. "Enemy sabotage; why don't we get those rats?" sighs the citizen as he folds up his newspaper.

Early in 1943, the army and navy noted this attitude of mind and issued a reassuring statement. Calculated in relation to passenger miles flown, the accident rate of military and naval aviation in the United States during 1942 was only a tiny fraction higher than the rate for commercial planes in normal years. The motto of civilian aviation is "safety first!" Even in the process of training, military aviation must sometimes say "safety last!" For example, in very bad weather the transcontinental lines ground their planes while the commanders of a training field deliberately send up students in order that they may learn to fly under some of the adverse conditions they will encounter in action. In view of this, these cold statistics refute the idea that there is any systematic sabotage of American aviation.

It is true that the F.B.I. and its auxiliaries have detected and punished several acts of sabotage by men of enemy-alien origin, or men influenced by enemy propaganda. Let the most clean-cut case stand for the rest. In 1941, the inspector at the Glenn Martin plant near Baltimore found that someone was damaging their bombers. The saboteur had no single method; but usually he cut wires or cables in the electrical system. Sometimes, however, he crushed hydraulic tubing or dropped into the gasoline tanks pieces of rubber cut from some other part of the plane. And once they found a card bearing the lettered legend "B-26, Martin's Death Trap—Heil Hitler!" This mysterious enemy had damaged twenty-four bombers before the F.B.I., by scientific inspection of tools, ran him down. He was a hitherto valued employee named Michael William Etzel, born in Baltimore of German parents, married, and with no criminal record. He had brooded on the alleged wrongs of the German people as set forth by Nazi propaganda until he determined to strike a blow against their enemies. A wide investigation failed to establish a connection with the Bund or any other German agency; almost certainly he was acting on his own initiative. Which fact did not prevent the court from sentencing him to fifteen years in the Federal Penitentiary. Other instances of deliberate sabotage, one by a sailor of Hungarian origin, one by an Italian-American, a few by men of German parentage, have boiled down to personal grudges against the management or fellow workmen, drunken impulses, and general no-accountness. Such cases of deliberate mischief occur even in periods of profound peace, and in all of those we have noted, the damage was trivial.

Why, after so many preliminary feints, did the Germans pull their punches? The authors have their own theory which they put forth humbly, admitting that they have little unimpeachable evidence to back it up.

As we all know, for five years before the war the Germans tried by agitation and propaganda to prevent us from supplying their enemies with munitions. In adopting this policy, they counted on practically unanimous support from the Teutonic element in the United States. True, the number of German born among us had shrunk greatly since 1918—slaves to statistics that they are, they could not have missed that fact. But as Nicolai reminded them, in the earlier war imperial Germany had only scratched the rich deposit of Teutonic sentiment in the second and third generation. With the Bund, with the old gag about Germany being a heaven, with promises that in the new world whose nucleus was the "New Europe" Germans would be a *Herrenvolk* and all the rest slaves, the Nazi propagandists tried to work the vein. New allies appeared in an American fifth column inspired by admiration of brute force, anti-Semitism, hatred for England, or the chance of profit in a new racket. Also, we had among us natives of countries like Hungary, Rumania, and Bulgaria, whose politicians were rapidly going fascist, whose governments were only biding their time to ally themselves peaceably with Germany. The Nazis spent much money, and with small returns, in trying to rouse them to action. Isolation was the slogan and peace the password. The Bund grew lyric over Germany's benevolent intentions toward the United States. Even the masters of Germany, so inept at divining any national psychology other than their own, could perceive that a single dramatic act of sabotage against an American ship or factory would give the lie to their propaganda. Quietly they organized for widespread destruction in America, but they held the forces of physical sabotage in reserve and played out the game of psychological sabotage to its disastrous end.

Meantime, our federal authorities had prepared against sabotage as thoroughly as against espionage. As soon as we began to manufacture new weapons for our enlarged army and navy, the F.B.I., at the request of military and naval intelligence, surveyed important war plants and suggested steps to insure greater protection. For at least a decade, all three organizations have been studying sabotage and countersabotage; and before long, ex-students of the German spy schools like William Sebold brought their knowledge of enemy methods up to date. They first looked over the sites and approaches of the factories and made suggestions as to the sealing or guarding of entrances outsiders might use to get at the machinery surreptitiously. They suggested that the vulnerable points in each plant be watched with special care. By circulars and private instruction they educated the management on the tricks and ruses of saboteurs. They stressed the importance of the rules, hitherto described, for looking into the past records and present loyalty of all old and new employees. In 1942 the army and navy assumed full responsibility for the investigation of employees and plant protection. The F.B.I. still investigates cases where sabotage and espionage are suspected. This is a great advance over the relatively haphazard methods of World War I.

Almost simultaneously, the coast guard took charge of protecting our ports against saboteurs. This in contrast with the corresponding period in the earlier war, when many munitions ships blew up or burned up in mid-Atlantic. Then, the shipping companies depended at first on the local police force or hired their own guards. In New York, German agents owned a controlling interest in an employment bureau that furnished many of the longshoremen. Even when the older F.B.I. took hold, lack of funds and personnel made it impossible to do a complete job of prevention. The coast guard, unlike the army and navy, does not merely train for war in time of peace. It fights a constant war of its own against ship-

wreck, marine disaster, storms, icebergs, smugglers and
harbor pirates. When in 1939 the President ordered our
sea police to supervise the loading of ships in our harbors,
they were trained and ready. The task grew beyond imagination. By 1943, we were sending troops, with their
supplies, to sixty-five foreign stations, to say nothing of
shipments of munitions to our allies. But, on official statement, we have lost not a single ship through sabotage in
our own ports, and there have been no equivalents of
Black Tom or other harbor explosions of the last war.

In this business of guarding against saboteurs, we
played in luck. In contrast to the situation during the
preliminaries to our other war, union labor was almost
unanimously with us. The A.F. of L. and the C.I.O. went
on record as being flatly and sternly opposed to Hitler
and all his works. No failure of the Germans was more
complete than their attempt to form pro-Axis labor
unions among the mechanics of Detroit. Between September 1, 1939, and June 22, 1941, the communist-
controlled unions played the German game but—probably upon orders—by hot propaganda and strikes, not by
sabotage. After Hitler double-crossed Stalin, they went
to the other extreme and began to give information on
potential saboteurs as well as actual spies. Union labor
as a whole became an army of counterspies who watched
wharves and factories like hawks for any sign of sabotage.

Pearl Harbor—and, as aforesaid, the F.B.I. laid hands
on the enemy agents whom they had been watching and
cataloguing for three years. Among them were hundreds

of Bundists and Nazi agents found working in munitions factories. Almost certainly these included the general staff and higher officers of the German army of sabotage in America. With its head chopped off, the creature died. Nevertheless the directors of our counterespionage waited in breathless apprehension. It seemed unlikely that spymasters so expert as the Germans had not provided a reserve corps. Also what about those foreign elements on whom the Nazis had spent so much money and effort? A few leaders, newly risen or still at large, might possibly stir them up to hamstring our sinews of war.

Both fears proved groundless. Apparently the Germans had provided no reserve force. Russian manpower and American manufacturing power will be the two main factors in our eventual triumph. And someday it may be written that when German intelligence underestimated the power of Russia and fumbled sabotage in America, it cleared the road to our victory. The old rule holds; the German secret services are still superficially clever and profoundly stupid.

As for the foreign born of enemy origin, they gave us another agreeable surprise. The German born and the sons and daughters of Germans had looked upon the coming war as an affectionate man looks upon an impending quarrel between his wife and his mother. He practices appeasement by instinct. But when the quarrel breaks, if he is normal and well married he sides with his wife. Within a week after Pearl Harbor, the German element —all but the 5 per cent already noted—were swarming into camp. The Italian born were almost unanimously with us, and soon the Attorney General removed them from the list of enemy aliens. The Hungarians—we interned only four of them—and on the average the Magyar people of the United States have given more money, more volunteers, and more service than has even the old original stock. Democracy has known no more heartening triumph.

Then in June, 1942, came a dramatic event which rightfully interpreted amounted to a confession of Nazi failure—the affair of the eight saboteurs. There were no effective saboteurs left in the United States; Germany was forced to import them. One significant paragraph in that twice-told story has escaped general attention. The capture of the four who landed on Long Island seemed like a fortunate accident. As they came ashore, they just happened to encounter coastguardsman Cullen who by native shrewdness saved his own life, divined their intentions, and put the F.B.I. on their trail. But what about the four who landed in Florida? No coastguardsman saw them land; yet within a week the F.B.I. had mysteriously found their cache of money and munitions and had captured the men themselves in a city a thousand miles away. This was the fact that chilled the masters of German sabotage. The operation was a kind of reconnaissance to determine the extent and efficiency of our watch for saboteurs. They learned! Moreover Germans of the dominance-mad class, like the Gestapo and the professional soldiers, interpret forbearance as weakness. We had never executed a spy since the Civil War. In peace as in war, spies against the "New Germany" had died at dawn by the headsman's axe while spies against us, after a long trial, had received mere sentences of imprisonment. But we not only executed six of these saboteurs by swift process of law, but condemned to death three men who had harbored them. Curious, but Uncle Sam had grown hard! As we write, nine months have passed since that episode on Amagansett Beach, and sabotage on our soil remains something to guard against but nothing more.

And the men who guard us against physical sabotage are not relaxing their vigilance. To do that would be to invite trouble. Most of them consider the present calm only a lull. They expect that the Germans will try again —next time perhaps not by a landing on our coasts but by some new route! Mexico is a perpetual anxiety. Recently her Falangist dissenters have grown more active. Her coasts and northern border are long and difficult to guard. Sabotage may break out when and where we least expect it.

More dangerous and more subtle than physical sabotage is psychological sabotage. "Divide minds and you can conquer bodies," was the motto of enemy agitation and propaganda in our period of hesitation. They tried to separate German-Americans from other Americans, white from black, Jew from Christian, republican from democrat, and to exaggerate division to such an extent that these groups flew at each other's throats. They had even built up a fairly large fifth column among native Americans. Even after Pearl Harbor, we let them go to extravagant lengths. Pelley had organized his Silver

Shirts in "cells" secret even from each other. Father Coughlin's *Social Justice* urged its readers to grab all the offices in the O.C.D. One speaker at a fifth-column meeting urged his hearers to "buy arms and keep them readily accessible," while another shouted, "Make the bloody purge of Hitler look like a picnic!" Still another used to show visitors a species of slung shot which he called the "kike-killer." In the Pelley trial, the prosecution proved that his publications were following almost slavishly the propaganda line of Herr Goebbels.

The Department of Justice long seemed cautious even to the point of timidity in its attitude toward these expressions and acts. But it was gathering evidence, and beginning in July, 1942, it brought a flock of indictments for plotting to cause mutiny in the armed forces and for other seditious offenses.

This sent the unindicted, including a lunatic fringe, scuttling to cover. And after Pearl Harbor the majority of the America First Society, composed of honest isolationists, lived up to the name by supporting the war earnestly and sincerely. The Axis agents and American fascists went into the silence.

But although the movement toward disruption had lost leadership and organization, it had not entirely lost its membership. Nazi propaganda based itself on the sound principle that hate is to certain temperaments an agreeable emotion. The circulation and influence of hundreds of Nazi-inspired publications between 1935 and 1941 prove that hundreds of thousands of Americans were indulging the luxury of hate and believing in bad fairies, and while they keep silence in public, they still express themselves in private. They constitute a nucleus which, as the war wears on the people, new enemy leadership and fresh propaganda may consolidate to create appeasement factions in our political parties, to lure us into accepting a premature peace (Pearl Harbor did not convert all of them), and finally to raise again the isolationist spirit, so that after the war we may repeat the tragic mistake of 1919, draw back into our shell, and twenty years later have a third World War to fight.

CHAPTER SEVEN

ARMY AND NAVY
INTELLIGENCE

THEY go by cryptic names: "G-2" and "O.N.I." Their
rather remote sanctuaries are barred by signs that warn:
NO PASSAGE; mostly, their doors are locked; their papers
stamped SECRET; their wastebaskets marked BURN. All of
which suggests mystery and glamor.

Now, mystery and glamor exist in military and naval
intelligence services, including the American. Yet much
of the mystery is not glamorous—"G-2" means simply
"General Staff, Army of the United States, Second Division"; "O.N.I." is "Office of Naval Intelligence"—and
much of the glamor is not mysterious. One who knows
says: "When we do a good job, it is not by hocus-pocus,
but by good American horse sense."

The "all-seeing I" of intelligence must not leer, but
gaze straight into the crystal ball if it is to see the truth
that a clever enemy tries to conceal; his strength and his
weakness, his prospects and his plans. For ignorant of
this truth, no general, no admiral can give battle safely
—and, in men's lives, cheaply. Mountbatten's Dieppe
raid might have succeeded fully had he known that a
German vessel, radio equipped, ready to warn, was cross-

ing his course. Eisenhower's landing in Africa might have failed without foreknowledge of tides and French defenses and politics.

Military and naval intelligence in action depend upon a minimum of hothouse intrigue and a maximum of cold courage: a scout who crawls through machine-gun fire to capture a prisoner for questioning; a pilot who touches the wheels of his plane to earth on an enemy airfield to photograph its hangars; a submarine commander who dodges nets and depth charges to reconnoiter a naval base.

All these things and more are part of a military intelligence service; so is a "secret service," employing spies and agents and counterspies. But there, too, the less hocus-pocus and the more common sense, the better. The Japanese spies, you will recall, pointed out Pearl Harbor's defenses not by cutting mysterious arrows in cane fields, but by just telling their diplomatically immune consulate. Americans and British have found that where the shooting is the artifices of espionage so famed in film and fable are often less effective than the equally fascinating but little-known battlefield detective work that forms a part of combat intelligence. This work, and all intelligence work, requires very special people, of very special talents.

An intelligence officer must have the imagination of a poet, rigidly controlled by the analytical ability of an insurance actuary. He is a rare bird, hybrid of woodpecker and hawk, able to plug or pounce. He may be a linguist, geographer, college professor, globe trotter, cryptographer. He must be as cautious as Fabius or as daring as MacArthur; either a teetotaler or copper lined, but never loose mouthed. He must toil to save his comrades' lives by ferreting out and telling them the enemy's secrets, while protecting their own secrets from the enemy.

Our intelligence chiefs are realists, preferring facts to figments. Major General George V. Strong has studied law and written a Japanese-American military dictionary; been military adviser at international disarmament conferences; mapped hemisphere defense as Chief of the General Staff's War Plans Division. He fought the Germans in 1918. His right-hand man, Brigadier General Hayes A. Kroner, is a former assistant military attaché in London. Rear Admiral Harold C. Train has also been a naval member of international disarmament conferences and has served on the Naval General Board. The navy knows Captain Ellis M. Zacharias as a leading expert on Japan, whose fluency in their language has helped in diplomacy and counterespionage in California and elsewhere, and who has fought and decisively beaten the Japs in the Pacific.

All these men know the enemy and can put themselves in his place. This mental reversal is so important that a British chief once made a group of intelligence officers wear their caps backward. In Washington today the core of the corps are regular officers of proven efficiency who have served in foreign countries, especially Axis or United Nations, and so know the true inwardness of enemy and friend.

Many of them have been military or naval attachés, officially representing the army or navy in the foreign country where they are "attached." In peacetime we lean upon them so heavily that some explanation in addition to that already given may be welcome. Through them friendly nations interchange such military information as they are willing to have known, about their strength, training, and armament. Attachés may attend maneuvers or be affiliated with regiments or ships. They must be good mixers, able to make well-informed friends.

The government to which an attaché is accredited knows all about this and facilitates it, so long as its own attachés enjoy similar courtesies. But it tries to control what foreign attachés see and learn. An American attaché visiting a Japanese regiment asked its colonel if he could see "the new machine gun."

"So sorry," said the colonel. "We have none."

A moment later they bumped into an excellent sample of the new machine gun. The colonel seized the attaché by the arm and whisked him away.

Thus rebuffed, the attachés of some foreign governments would have resorted to bribery or spying. Some nations cynically term their own attachés "official spies" and, believing that foreigners must be the same, tap their telephones and otherwise spy on them.

This country, however, has depended in peacetime so largely upon open and aboveboard attachés and so little upon spies that Mussolini once laughingly remarked that the Americans must have the best military espionage system in the world, for no one had been able to discover it. To his devious mind we seemed naïve. To ourselves, we seemed horse-sensible, for if we got less information than nations more Machiavellian, also we got less mis-information. We supplemented official data from sources like American bankers and businessmen with foreign contacts, travelers, and journalists—who sometimes were also reserve officers. They gave information not for hire but as a patriotic duty. We believed that an informant who has to be paid is, like a woman of the same sort, not the best. Also we leaned heavily upon swapping informa-tion until, by 1938, the swap became a swindle, at least with the Axis Powers.

Three years before Pearl Harbor, the O.N.I. asked the Japanese for some details of the new cruisers they were building.

"We can tell you nothing," said the Japs.

"Then," objected O.N.I., "we can tell you nothing of our new Naval Aviation program."

"No matter," retorted the Japs. "We can read it all in your newspapers or Congressional Record."

Which was all too true. In order to get even a little money, the services had to tell Congress—and hence the world—much that our potential enemy wanted to know.

We have indicated that the term "military secret" is elastic. It may include anecdotes indicating how generals and admirals will act in a pinch. The Gamelin fiasco of 1940 did not surprise informed Americans. A whole range of secrets is indicated by these fundamentals that any naval intelligence seeks to know:

Construction and performance of enemy warships;

radius of action and speed; armor and armament, their character and distribution; gunnery; fire control; communications systems; recognition signals; training—for instance, in night attack—and over-all plans of operation; also data on coastal waters, tides, and currents.

To gather the last named, the Japanese used the powerful motor "fishing boats" we have already described, often manned by naval reservists. They were operated from American harbors and usually owned by Japanese having American citizenship. Our Japanese population, while more loyal than most Americans believe, afforded recruits and concealment for spying in a white man's country not enjoyed by the far fewer white men in a yellow man's country. Since Pearl Harbor we have greatly augmented our knowledge of Japan, but before that infamous day we did not know that their aircraft carriers were rehearsing the attack—probably among the Mandated Islands the Japanese had made virtually spyproof. Nor did our files show that the Japanese had so many carriers.

All war and navy departments amass vast stores of facts, being by location and other means safe enough to protect them. These facts are filed mostly by countries and strategic areas. There may be an "Eur-African Group," a "Far Eastern Group," a "German Desk," or a "Japanese Desk." At these desks sit men who are authorities on those countries or regions. They weigh and classify the information so that it becomes readily available in whatever circumstances arise. G-2's "Strategic Index" aims to answer 484 different questions about the war potential of a foreign country, military, naval, economic, political, and moral. In peacetime the General Staff's War Plans Division uses this data to prepare plans for every possible strategic eventuality of wartime. But when war comes, the best-laid plans must be adapted to unforeseen circumstances.

Military and naval intelligence now receive some 250,-000 communications daily. In peacetime they got more real help from the American Geographic Society or the Museum of Natural History than from all the spies in Hollywood. In wartime they turn to thousands of professional societies as well as individuals for information about coastal currents, inland topography, soil, underground and surface water conditions, from the ends of the earth to the ends of the earth.

They tap former residents of foreign countries, including foreign-born Americans, for a wide variety of information. They assemble photographs "of everywhere from everywhere," including vacationers' snapshots. Before British commandos raided Bruneval, France, they selected from an extensive file one of a beach with parked automobiles, the other of a cliff topped by a road and a fence. The pictures showed they could land automobiles on the beach, and how to reach their objective. Such a file is now being assembled here by the Office of Strategic Services, which under Colonel William J. Donovan performs special duties of preparing data for the two intelligence services. Its photographic experts are gathering and correlating photographs of many strategic areas in the world.

In peacetime, too, intelligence services gather data—
from official sources, such as government and consular
reports, trade journals, and commercial and banking
establishments with foreign ramifications—on the industrial capacity of all potential enemy nations. And how
about the manpower of the same nations; its quantity
and quality? Calculations include every factor, such as
new medical developments like the use of blood plasma
and sulfa drugs that have greatly reduced deaths from
wounds. Intelligence services must also know of conditions that may affect the morale of troops—as in France.

Studying enemy newspapers is useful even in wartime
despite the rigorous Nazi censorship, and even because
of it. It may show what they want us to think. Sometimes it allows bits of military information to be put together, matching a paragraph from Berlin with a sentence
from Munich. The simple statement: "The fete was en-
livened by the music of the Guards' band," revealed the
whereabouts of a certain Guards Division because there
were only five and we knew where the other four were.
Newspapers indicate the state of morale, and in the winter of 1942–43 the proportion of death notices that said
"Died for the Führer" has gone way down. Now they just
die for the Fatherland. The big British raid on Rostock
was greatly aided by a German magazine article describing the city's growth as an aircraft center.

The development of that raid as described by Air Vice
Marshal Charles E. H. Medhurst illustrates the vision of
"the eyes of I." Those eyes, first attracted by that magazine article, searched the newspapers of Rostock for such

items as (1) new workers' quarters; (2) head of a local factory reports expansion; (3) a businessman from Rostock is in Switzerland recruiting skilled workers on precision instruments; (4) a report from Latin America that a Rostock manufacturer has canceled an order for his goods; (5) special search of prisoners from Rostock shows letters saying that their women are getting jobs in "the new factories."

So if there are fixed-post spies in Rostock, they are told to send full information; if not, spies are sent there. So are air photographers with telescopic equipment with which, thirty thousand feet up at three hundred miles an hour, they can take photographs that will reveal railroad ties. Closer-ups can be supplied by flying back and forth at different times of the day and at different heights and angles, using a plane stripped of all extra weight to make from four hundred to five hundred miles an hour. These planes are painted to be virtually invisible when diving, with the sun behind them, so fast that antiaircraft guns cannot catch them.

The film is put together into a mosaic. It is touched up and enlarged to reveal not only lights, shades, and contours but enemy camouflage. The resulting map is studied by experts in interpretation and supplied to bomber crews before they take off. Then they are "briefed" by intelligence officers, with all other information available about Rostock. When they come back, the same intelligence officers pump them on what they saw and where: landmarks, camouflage, decoys, fires, antiaircraft guns, searchlights, and, above all, new enemy tactics. Then the aerial photographers return to photograph the damage: wrecked factories and panicky crowds thronging railroad stations. Their snapshots of the French fleet, sunk at Toulon, showed the extent of damage. After Pacific naval battles, our cameras check on enemy ships.

The camera's flying eye is completing a unique service not only for war but for peace as well by photographing areas not fully mapped. Neither the army nor the navy can safely proceed without good maps, which for combat must show contour and details—not only railroads and telegraph lines, but lighthouses, churches, and any cover for troops including cemeteries. Composite maps showing the whereabouts of all units, friendly and enemy, are closely guarded. The navy prints over two million a month, and has prepared charts of three thousand separate areas of the world, including some charts that enable fliers to land safely in totally unfamiliar and obscure places.

Gathering data for them is an adventurous aspect of intelligence work. European intelligence services have camouflaged mapmaking surveys as archaeological expeditions. Today in far places our mapmakers brave wild beasts, wild men, weather, and disease. These last two play a part in intelligence work. Medical intelligence investigates conditions affecting the health of troops, from water supply to jungle fever. The Nazi invasion of France was preceded by careful weather calculations. It is no accident that our Pacific task forces have had thick weather to screen their approach to their objectives, but once arrived, clear weather.

Radio and aviation are playing an ever-increasing role as the "eyes of I." Radio location has made great strides. Airmen flying over the front, be it land or sea or from balloon, spy targets not for bombing alone but also for artillery shelling, or spot fortifications, or movements of troops or ships. The navy's scout planes detected a Japanese task force steaming for the Solomons in time to give us a spectacular victory.

These reports may come by photograph or by voice hoarse with combat over the radiotelephone, which after air power and photography is the biggest intelligence development of this war. It played an unappreciated part in making possible the movements of the German blitzkrieg, so rapid that they could not be forestalled, even though, to save time in encoding and decoding, the Nazis spoke in "clear"; "all planes to Abbeville!" New types of radio telephone may even end the famous "fog of war" that hitherto has stifled commanders and staffs in delayed, incomplete, or contradictory news of how the battle went.

The staccato reports of fliers, coming in to carriers or land bases, best enable intelligence officers to keep on a big chart a running picture with notes and tables of an action being fought hundreds of miles away. One of the jeep's virtues is that it can take a radiotelephone to so many places quickly.

Often, the jeep riders are also trained in scouting—can find their way by moss on tree trunks or tell by a truck's tire tracks where it is going. Observers are trained to see through glasses from swaying tree top or fighting top, to catch the farthest glint of sun on steel or telltale smoke haze, to report every tiniest detail that shows where the enemy is busiest and at what. Some observers catch the flash or sound of artillery fire and calculate the whereabouts of the guns. Still others intercept radio messages between enemy ships or ground forces. As we have explained elsewhere, these messages may, under the tender ministrations of the cryptanalysts, afford valuable information of enemy movements and intentions. Intelligence taps enemy telephone conversations, if only because new voices mean that new troops have arrived, which G-2 wants to know.

Every enemy division is indexed: where it came from, where it has fought, and how well. A shock division? What are they up to? To find out, specially trained officers just ask them. For the deepest "secret" of combat intelligence in all armies is this common-sense fact: the most reliable news comes, not from hocus-pocus, but from the expert questioning of prisoners and the sifting of captured papers. This information is fresher, more reliable, more easily checked than spy reports.

Movies indicate that the commando's foremost purpose is to stick a knife into a Nazi's back, but actually it is to bring that Nazi back alive to be searched and questioned. In 1917 our first German prisoner resisted, was bayoneted and died without telling that his comrades were then rehearsing the first German raid on American troops, which was a surprise—and a success.

Expertly handled prisoners told us virtually every major German move of 1918, offensive or defensive. They foretold, step by step, the German defense throughout our greatest battle, the Meuse-Argonne, from the Prussian Guards' first counterattack to the whereabouts of the final line of resistance.

The unique intelligence group who got these results were the A.E.F.'s most effective "secret service." Their chief, Major Sanford Griffith, had lived in a German garrison town. They included Milwaukee German-Americans and a Lutheran minister. Even among themselves they spoke German and ate German food, the better to understand their human material and extract from it that precious commodity: military intelligence.

We used no concentration-camp methods but sound psychology. We did not baby our prisoners; we frankly took advantage of their shocked, depressed state; but we treated them as human beings, each with his peculiarities. During questioning they were not made to stand stiffly at attention.

"Would you like us to send word via Switzerland to your family that you're safe?"

Anger or fright began to melt.

"Well, how's the beer in Munich now?"

A little more joking, and then with a grin:

"Does Major Schmalz still stick down in that deep dugout?"

Ach Gott! thought the prisoner. He even knows about my battalion commander—the big *Lump!* This *Amerikaner's* pretty wise. Why not answer? He isn't taking notes.

But behind a panel someone was; a German-American who knew German shorthand.

At first, three quarters of the captured officers refused information or lied. But they yielded to the personal touch of former German officers who had joined forces with G-2. Some were Alsatians, some socialists. Unobtrusively they mingled with officers in the cages, making mental notes. One graduate of an officers' school pumped the staff officers. A bandaged aviator mingled with captured airmen. Some expertly sifted the truths from orders, diaries, and letters captured from German dugouts or pockets. A boy lieutenant had an entire German defense plan. Other papers gave antitank tactics, locations of battery positions. The letters told of shortages of food and of morale at home; the diaries, of morale and troop movements at the front.

We are using the same methods today, with improvements based upon the latest psychological research.

The Japanese are brave but excitable, and not immune to enlightened intelligence methods. We have persuaded some to desert by loudspeaker promises of good food. Their officers assure them we will kill them if they surrender, but when they find this to be untrue, they not infrequently respond to fair treatment. A few are even willing to tell their comrades of this treatment by loudspeaker or pamphlet. Since war began, the information willingly furnished by deserters has been especially valuable, and new methods are continually being sought to encourage desertion. German deserters gave information that helped make St. Mihiel an American victory. In Africa they and the Italians are just beginning to come over to our lines, bearing our leaflets advising them to do so.

We opened this winter a direct attack upon the morale of Japanese soldiers by dropping from airplanes leaflets shaped physically and psychologically to appeal to their sentimental side and their devotion to the Emperor. One leaflet, shaped like the Asiatic paulownia leaf says: "Before spring comes again the bombs of America will fall like paulownia leaves, bringing misfortune and bad omen. The fall of one such leaf is a portent of the annihilation of the militarists." Another, shaped like a tung leaf, quotes a poem by the Emperor: "Beautiful are the days of peace." Both suggest to Japanese fighting men that they are fighting for militarists who have overruled their sacred Emperor.

Italian prisoners frequently are helpful, especially when questioned by antifascist Italians. Not a few Nazis respond to careful treatment. A Russian intelligence report says: "Veterans among the prisoners complain of the quality of recruits their units have been receiving." Letters the Russians captured last winter traced a progressive decline in German morale. The British got an order by an Italian general rebuking parachutists for refusing to jump. Scouts are trained to search not only enemy dugouts but enemy dead as well for papers and even insignia identifying their units.

Travelers and refugees from enemy or occupied territory are another good source of information. Intelligence officers accompany advancing troops and, aided by former residents of the region, question all civilians who may have learned anything. Travelers arriving in Sweden and Portugal from Germany are the object of earnest if concealed interest. In battle areas civilians are asked: "What regiment was in your village? How heavy were their casualties? Did any of them curse Hitler? How many?"

The battlefield yields valuable information about the enemy's weapons: guns, tanks, ammunition. Specialists examine them, eagerly seeking something new. Specimens are tested for new ideas, for comparison with our own and for defensive measures.

Air intelligence services always ask: "Any new enemy kites today?" And if a new type of plane is reported, orders go out: "Knock one down so we can take it apart." To prevent that, the Japanese for some time pursued every falling Zero to earth and bombed and machine-gunned it, regardless of the crews. The Japs lost nearly a hundred Zeros in finding out that we had put a tail gun on our Flying Fortress bomber. Once a new weapon or a new type is spotted, air intelligence wants to know whence it is operated and so where it will hit us.

Naval intelligence relies considerably on undersea power. Our submarines that sink ships in Japanese harbors also report on ship and convoy movements and ship-yard activities. One submarine commander viewed a war-ship launching. The torpedoing of the British battleship *Royal Oak* involved submarine spying and illustrated how "I" watches naval bases.

A German naval officer who had long conducted a watch-repair shop near Scapa Flow found two openings in the entrance nets. He sent word via a "letter drop" in Holland; then, in a rubber boat he piloted the sub-marine through one of the openings. Submarines have transported commandos on expeditions seeking informa-tion, and saved from Corregidor American intelligence officers marked for death by the Japanese.

Thus from all sources army and navy intelligence con-stantly receive information—and misinformation. To find out which is which, the whole influx must always be "evaluated and interpreted" by experts who check and double check. Suppose a fixed-post spy at a German headquarters sends this report: "First panzer division moving via Y to X. Attacks in 10 days."

Beside that report G-2 places another in which a "train watcher" at Y reports as passing through Y, thirty-five trains of sixty-five cars—the number and type for a panzer division. But has the unit time to reach X, de-train, deploy, and attack?

Officers specializing in troop movement compare train and march tables. Yes, perhaps it has. So planes seek and bomb the trains and the routes they are using, while ground reinforcements are moved toward X.

However sharply it may gaze into the crystal ball, can

intelligence predict the future? Yes, usually. Had O.N.I. been unhampered, it could have known more about Japanese aircraft carriers. It has foreseen many Japanese moves. No American service has perpetrated a blunder equaling the Nazis' failure to know how wide open to invasion Britain was in 1940, or the Japs' failure to know that Hawaii was just as wide open after Pearl Harbor. However, politicians of all nations—especially Hitler—often ignore their experts' predictions.

Intelligence forewarns the fighting fronts or fleets, coast defenses or training areas, by courier, army mail, air, wire, or radio. Facsimile transmission of messages, maps, and photographs over thousands of miles has developed into a tremendous aid. Intelligence also prepares for the troops circulars on various enemy methods. Its publications are mostly "secret, confidential, or restricted," which is one form of military counterespionage.

"Counterespionage," said an expert, "results from the danger of spies being everywhere." That includes the ranks and areas of the army and navy. From training camp and navy yard to scene of battle, G-2 and O.N.I. fight espionage, sabotage, and subversion by tactics defensive and offensive. This did not really begin until 1936, when this innocent country was a spy's paradise.

The Axis, preparing for war, began concerted efforts to pick the smart Yankee scientific brains of secrets of new guns and antitank weapons, or how the navy launches and retrieves scouting planes. One power paid ten thousand dollars for a gas-mask secret; another tried to steal one of the famous crystal clocks wherewith the Naval Observatory regulates the nation's time to three one-thousandths of a second. The Japanese haunted our Patent Office and Bureau of Standards. The Germans got from us dive bombers and paratroopers and bought for fifteen cents from the Government Printing Office our carefully worked out Industrial Mobilization Plan which now enables them to prolong their resistance.

Not until after Pearl Harbor did we really slam the door. But when at Midway Japanese airmen ran into American planes with new features secretly installed, they fell like leaves. So counterespionage helps in a battle. It could have done more and sooner but for a skeptical public and Congress. The army's appropriation was a few thousand dollars, and large areas were covered by "one colonel, one sergeant, and one typewriter"—and important German spies escaped. Naval counterespionage was better, though insufficiently financed, and more widespread. December, 1941, found two hundred intelligence officers in the West, where for years they had been opposed by an aggressive enemy—Japanese naval intelligence.

Their fishing-boat spies were so persistent in photographing, mapping, sounding, and shadowing our Pacific Fleet, that it was ordered long before Pearl Harbor to fire on or capture them. In New York their "Purchasing Commission" maintained an office whose door was marked "I.J.N." (Imperial Japanese Navy) where officers clipped every naval item from newspapers and technical journals, and whence they issued to photograph bases and cruisers.

In 1938 all photographing was forbidden at twenty defense areas. Soon after Pearl Harbor, Japanese were evacuated from the coast inland, and many more military areas were barred from sunset to sunrise to civilians or to anyone without a special permit, and residents were forbidden to have explosives, radio transmitters, maps, or drawings.

Military and naval intelligence begin with his induction the soldier's or sailor's education in keeping his mouth shut and his writing finger under control. First they teach him what is military information valuable to the enemy; then, how to protect it.

Censorship on letters from training camp is justified if it succeeds only in curing the recruit's longing to tell his loved ones where he—and hence his unit—is. One disgusted officer wrote to a soldier's girl:

DEAR MISS BLANK:

Your boy-friend still loves you but he writes too much.

THE CENSOR

In 1942 the army amused the country by decreeing that a string of X's for kisses was henceforth forbidden. But it was a sensible regulation. The number and arrangement of "kisses" might constitute a code.

Censoring of military mail is more important now than in any previous war. The microphotographic V-letters come home by airplane, affording fresher news than in 1918; and we cannot too often repeat that in espionage rapid transmission is frequently the essential factor. Soldiers are taught not to write to or answer letters from people unknown to them, or join "correspondence clubs"—an old spy trick.

And there *are* spies in the services. In January, one offered five hundred dollars for an army code. One soldier received thirty-four hundred dollars for information on aviation; others, lesser sums for data on transport movements. Spies in the army and navy are usually arrested by the F.B.I., but largely on evidence unearthed by the army's counterintelligence or the navy's similar force. Those are the real secret services and do not appear in court.

Whoever enters this "legion that never was 'listed' " becomes anonymous. He is chosen for initiative, toughness, and investigative experience. Many operatives speak several languages—one speaks thirteen—and they include all colors, creeds, and ages. Nine applicants out of ten are rejected. The remainder are trained "to shoot, to shadow, to stick." Spyhunting is mostly detail and drudgery, asking questions, watching, and waiting. Thirty-two thousand pieces of mail were checked to track a subversive "Mothers' " group. Also, there is danger.

An operative, seeking saboteurs on an army construction job, saw a shadow whizzing toward him, turned and ducked a heavy Stilson wrench dropped from above. Having been spotted, he was replaced by three other operatives. They got the man who had dropped the wrench.

They operate wherever the army is—Guadalcanal, Iceland, Africa—hunting spies or the disloyal. Sometimes they work in uniform, often in civilian clothes. They ignore criminal cases, which the military police handle. Naval counterespionage protects the myriad warships now building from spies and saboteurs. The coast guard investigates all water-front workers before granting identity cards. Crews of all nations are checked, especially radio operators. Seamen are allowed only one type of receiving set; for all others, even when receiving Amos 'n Andy, emit radiations revealing their whereabouts to submarines.

To prevent submarines from landing spies or getting information of ship movements, beaches are patrolled by horsemen. Observers are stationed in ports, in balloons, and planes, including civilian volunteers. The air patrol detected a schooner, her decks laden with oil drums, threading Caribbean keys. Search of her crew revealed stolen plans of our Panama Naval Air Station. But all told, German espionage on shipping here is barely semi-efficient.

Military counterespionage comprises mostly defensive methods of preventing the enemy from finding out the truth about one's own forces, movements, and intentions, such as removing ship names from sailors' hatbands. But counterespionage may take the offensive to make the enemy believe an untruth or otherwise baffle him. A common way is to drop misinformation into the gaping ears of newspapermen who write articles that the enemy must waste time and spies investigating.

But beyond that: British naval intelligence trapped a German squadron at the Falkland Islands by sending fake orders in a captured German code, and tied up by law suit or other pretext every tanker the Nazis had in South America to fuel the *Graf Spee*. An American intelligence officer in a hotel known as a spies' resort wrote an "Official Report" on preparations for an attack supposed to be contemplated far from the real one, then threw the fresh carbon paper with the words clearly stenciled into the wastebasket and left the room. Returning, he found the carbon paper gone, and the Germans' subsequent actions showed they had been fooled. We sent an expedition to Greenland to catch spies who were radioing to Germany weather forecasts for use in bombing Britain. And the Nazis are said to have allowed faked plans of their 1940 offensive to fall into Belgian hands.

Having examined the details of the G-2–O.N.I. picture, we can get the perspective by reconstructing what intelligence did to make successful the North African expedition, the biggest overseas invasion in history. It was decided upon in July, 1942, but for a year twenty-odd American "observers" had been in North Africa to supervise shipments of American goods—and to make contact with French patriots and collect information, political, military, and economic.

In this country, libraries supplied books, maps, even city directories of North Africa. Nine volumes were prepared on resources, engineering problems, railroads, roads, water supply. The Casablanca reservoir was among our first objectives. The R.A.F. made many air photographs and we printed several thousand different ones. The capacity of ports was calculated.

Weather experts picked November 8 as the best day to land troops and equipment through the heavy ground swell; also it was the end of the month when Mohammedans had fasted, and the beginning of one when they were not supposed to fight.

Hundreds of British agents wended the narrow alleys of Algiers, Rabat and Oran, making contact with patriotic Frenchmen. They prepared for the submarine expedition of Lieutenant General Clark to meet prominent French officers willing to aid the landing. While police searched their rendezvous, Americans and British waited in the cellar, fingers on triggers. They escaped by submarine, and while they lost eighteen thousand dollars in gold, they had left behind thirty-two thousand. Perhaps the thirty-two thousand dollars helped our fliers and paratroops to land unopposed on Algerian airfields. Thanks to another submarine exploit, the French General Giraud joined General Eisenhower just in time to appeal to the French to aid the Americans and British. This was done over a powerful long-wave transmitter aboard an American battleship, supplemented by President Roosevelt's speaking through fifty transmitters and by leaflets dropped from planes.

Our troops were welcomed by Frenchmen who guided them toward batteries and fortifications whose location was already marked on the numerous different maps the troops carried. Yet, as we have seen, the Axis, though knowing an expedition was bound somewhere, did not know where. The reason was Allied counterespionage measures.

Four months earlier ten staff officers, discussing the plan behind guarded doors, used instead of place names not even code words, but gestures. G-2 set aside "Africa" offices where visitors, stenographers, even carbons were forbidden. Everything was written in longhand. Lest news of large orders for supplies reach the enemy, they were spread among many purchasing offices and depots. Shipments were marked with code symbols; names of British ports meant African ports. Thousands of maps were printed of other and misleading objectives.

Staff officers were sent elsewhere to "arrange for American troop movements," and the news "leaked" to that world spy center, Lisbon. Articles hinting at an attack on Dakar appeared in American publications. A public-relations officer let correspondents see him studying Russian, and some correspondents boarded transports not in tropical but in winter uniforms. Newspapers here were told that General Eisenhower had returned to "confer" in Washington, and in New York messages were left for him at several places that are gossip centers.

With the troops landed intelligence agents who had been trained in questioning prisoners. Others were ready to guard the Spanish-Moroccan border against Axis spy couriers en route to Spain and Hitler; to checkmate Axis efforts to hire Moroccan bandits to harass us.

German intelligence was furious. We had beaten them at a game at which they considered themselves masters: the co-ordination of all methods of warfare, conventional and unconventional. Nevertheless, our intelligence service considers theirs a formidable opponent and takes seriously the increasing attention their espionage is paying us.

And our espionage? The reader has seen that it is but a part of military and naval intelligence, and not infrequently a minor part. The drama is less of complicated plots and glamorous sirens than of devoted men and women daring death at dawn before a firing squad, to toil at a laborious task like counting trains.

Yet in all our wars military and naval espionage have played a part. General Clark's expedition to Africa is not unprecedented. Our victory over Spain in 1898 owed much to two secret missions. A naval officer, Henry H. Ward, disguised as a yachtsman, reported the movements of the Spanish fleet, and an army officer, Ralph H. Van Deman, spied out the land of Cuba and changed the plans for our invasion. And our agents helped start the revolutions in Germany and Austria-Hungary with which World War I ended.

We have tried to set military espionage in its proper perspective, yet to indicate that it has certain major uses:

At an enemy headquarters, to report plans and future moves.

In rear areas, to report troop movements under way; fortifications and targets for bombing; output of old and new equipment.

At base ports and naval bases, to report movements of warships or cargo vessels.

Everywhere—to report on morale.

Wherever he be, the spy or the intelligence officer is no more valuable than his own wits and his means of communication. And there is where we Americans come in. We are aided by our progress in mastering modern methods of collecting and transmitting military and naval intelligence—aviation, radio photography—and by our wealth of recruits among the millions of loyal Americans born in every country on earth, including the Axis countries. Our relative inexperience is counterbalanced by shrewdness, imagination, initiative, and adaptability. We can build the best intelligence service in the world—and the best secret service.

CHAPTER EIGHT

WHAT CAN THE CITIZEN DO ABOUT IT?

THE loyal citizen may well ask himself that question. He knows that spies, saboteurs, and rumormongers are dangerous enemies whom he may encounter right at home, anywhere from Portland, Maine, to Portland, Oregon. He wants to help his government crush these enemies, yet when he considers the complexities of secret service he feels like a man confronted with a crossword puzzle in Sanskrit.

There are, however, several things that the citizen can do about it, and his government wants him to do them. It is true that the F.B.I. has received from citizens letters telling how Japanese disguised as salmon were swimming up the Columbia River, and German spies were communicating with one another through water faucets. But it is also true that the F.B.I. has received from citizens letters that in the first ten months since Pearl Harbor resulted in the detection of thousands of hostile enemy aliens, with arms, explosives, and short-wave radios. The "spot raids" that you read about daily result very largely from letters from citizens. Some of those letters are hysterical nonsense, some are malicious spite work, but a surprising proportion are of genuine value. Since a fundamental of counterespionage is to build up as many reliable sources of information as possible, government agencies encourage all loyal and responsible citizens to help.

The reader has seen that counterespionage not only hunts spies and saboteurs, but guards against leaks of information from which they may profit. Everyone, man, woman, and child, can help do that. And in wartime, too little secrecy may cost lives, but too much hardly can.

A subordinate of Admiral Canaris submitted a memorandum saying there were so many secrecy regulations that they were slowing up Germany's war effort. Canaris endorsed the memorandum: "Strictly Secret." That sounds ridiculous, but the Nazi master spy was demonstrating another principle of counterespionage: "Who knows just what is a military secret to the enemy? Why hand him any information he can possibly use? Why help him kill your men and prolong the war? Better to make him work for what he gets and worry and use spies that otherwise he would use elsewhere. Make him no present of information." That is more easily done than seems possible. Members of the Duquesne spy ring testified that they picked up valuable bits that were let fall in talk at bridge games and bars. On New Year's Day a New Yorker was arrested for showing restaurant acquaintances a manifest sheet detailing names, cargoes, and sailing dates of ships. Yet on Christmas Day the Office of Censorship had issued this appeal: "Do not tell the names of ships upon which sailors serve."

Here are complete and official instructions headed DON'T TALK:

1. ABOUT TROOPS:

>Location, except for troops in training and on police duty.
>
>Where, when, or how troop movements will be made.
>
>Characteristics and limitations of equipment or weapons.
>
>Concentration or special training of units.

2. ABOUT HARBORS, SHIPS, AND CARGOES:

>Location, destination or cargo of United States, Allied or neutral vessels.
>
>*Any* information about a transport, convoy, harbor defense, or mine field.
>
>Construction or proposed launchings.
>
>Condition and setup of shipyards.
>
>Sinking or damage until officially announced.

3. ABOUT DAMAGE:

>Generally speaking, do not disclose any information in your possession as to damage done to our side by any action of the enemy.

4. ABOUT AIRPLANES:

>Production of any plant or number in any military unit.
>
>Location, destination, or time of departure of air units.
>
>Troop movements or war material shipment by air.
>
>Characteristics and limitations.

Development or experiment.

Name, plans, or orders of members of Air Transport Command.

5. ABOUT FORTIFICATIONS AND ANTIAIRCRAFT INSTALLATIONS:

Location and description.

Location of bomb shelters or camouflaged objects or other defense precautions.

Any information of United States installations outside the United States.

6. ABOUT PRODUCTION:

Don't give out any information on production known to you. Let the other fellow get what he's supposed to know out of the newspapers.

7. ABOUT WEATHER:

Don't pass on information of weather conditions other than that which appears in your local newspaper.

8. ABOUT RUMORS AND HARMFUL STORIES:

Don't repeat stories—

That stir up racial discussion.

Inimical to our friendship with or in criticism of our allies.

Of the enemy's prowess.

Of our inefficiencies or shortcomings.

About shortage or poor quality of our equipment.

Challenge all rumors.

To keep such things from the enemy, the nation has

been papered with posters, one of which expresses the theme of all: DON'T BE A BLABBOTEUR!

"We forget," the army warns its recruits, "that the enemy agent, if he is to be successful and avoid a firing squad, must be such a plausible and convincing person that no one suspects him. He will look exactly like what he isn't: a typical American with an honest face who knows as much about the Yankees and the Brooklyn Dodgers as we do. Enemy agents are quiet, hard-working investigators who go about using their ears and eyes, picking up a little item here and another there by encouraging people to say more than they should."

The average citizen should not let himself be encouraged or encourage others. The army believes that the most common cause of blabbing is conceit. "Why do we boast?" it asks, and replies: "Most of us, to impress a woman. A popular girl is a good listener. So is a spy." How fortunate it is that not so many women are blabboteurs as some men suppose! For three years, more than a thousand women have known the secret of how Britain locates spy radios, but not one woman has revealed it, or even indicated that there is a secret to reveal.

But here is "the hardest security lesson to learn": Military information must be shared with *no one,* not even with those you love. They may give it away without knowing they have done so.

As our own war effort expands, practically everyone will at some time have in his or her possession some information that will be of value to the enemy—some little item some spy would like to pick up. This is especially true of those immediately connected with the defense effort, and those living in special defense areas. But it also includes all who have relatives or friends in such work or in the armed services.

So be careful of what you say or what you repeat; especially, do not repeat anything you hear—true or untrue —about spies, sabotage, or fifth-column activities. To do so may spread warning or panic. Also, be careful where you say it. The army finds that its recruits, who are typical Americans, believe too implicitly in the safety of the United States mail and telephone and telegraph services —also in the discretion of their fellow men.

Soldiers and sailors, new ones especially, talk enough about military matters without being encouraged by civilians. If you encounter service men—and that includes officers—who talk too freely, try tactfully to caution them, and if this fails, report them, giving name and unit, time and place, and other details of importance, to the War Department, Washington, D.C. But it may work both ways. The boys are learning, and if you seem too inquisitive, they may report you. They may even swing on you; it has happened. They have been warned against strangers who offer them drinks or automobile rides and then ask questions, as Ludwig and other spies have done.

If service men write you military information, don't broadcast it, even if it has been passed by the censor. He is only human, may be wrong, and what is harmless information in one part of the globe may be harmful in another. And don't write letters to service men you don't know—especially if you are of the feminine gender. Few will answer you, for it is against orders, and those who do may be court-martialed. They have been warned that women spies write such letters. They may turn in your letter, which means an investigation that will be troublesome for you and for an overworked staff. Also, when writing service men you know, don't try some secret "code"—or allow them to. Expert cryptographers will readily solve the "secret," and, again, you and your correspondent will probably get into trouble. Last, if you are a draft registrant, you will save everyone trouble by following instructions promptly and fully, and always keeping your registration card with you.

The patriotic citizen will readily see that the more people take the measures of defensive counterespionage just outlined, the less work for our counterspies and the more work for enemy spies. But what American is satisfied with mere defense against an invisible enemy? All want to know what they can do about the disloyal, about saboteurs and spies they may encounter. Yet every American, appreciating how thoroughly the F.B.I. and other government agencies investigate every plausible complaint or bit of information, wishes to avoid sending in reports of Japanese disguised as salmon or parachutists landing unless he has really seen the salmon or the parachutist. They are equally fabulous. Literally hundreds of parachutist reports have been investigated, and none

has been found true. The "parachutes" have been everything from sleeve targets towed by airplanes to rubber
toys made in Japan.

Here are two other hardy perennials:

1. *The ground-glass story:* Saboteurs are putting it
into various edible things—lately, cans of shrimp. The
F.B.I.'s technical laboratory found the glass was a few
crystals of struvite or magnesium ammonium phosphate,
a constituent of canned sea food that is normal and harmless.

2. *The "lights-flashing" story:* German spies are signaling one another by flashing lights. Often the "flashes"
are caused by a flapping window curtain or a boy blink-
ing a flashlight at his girl friend across the way.

A moment's reflection will show that flashing lights
are a mode of signaling that is very risky to try, and actually seldom tried anywhere but on the seashore. And
that moment's reflection will mark the difference between a valuable volunteer informant and an hysterical
nuisance—also between reasonable precaution and un-
just suspicion or persecution of foreigners. The vast majority here, even of Axis-Americans, have proven their
loyalty. However, anyone, of whatever race or descent,
who parrots the Axis propaganda line is naturally worth
reporting. So is anyone who opposes the draft or the sale
of defense bonds. No democracy fighting for its life can
allow license of speech and remain a democracy. Things
that "go" in peacetime, do not "go" in wartime. Our
Constitution and laws recognize that.

Nevertheless, there are still loopholes in our laws against peacetime espionage, despite some pre-Pearl Harbor efforts by Congress to plug them piecemeal. We need a single, comprehensive counterespionage law, good in peace or war. For war, our mainstay is the Act of June 15, 1917. It says:

> Whoever, in time of war, with intent that the same shall be communicated to the enemy, shall collect, record, publish or communicate or attempt to elicit any information with respect to the movement, numbers, description or condition or disposition of any of the armed forces, ships, aircraft or war materials of the United States . . . or intended for the fortification or defense of any place, or any other information relating to the public defense which might be useful to the enemy, shall be punished by death or by imprisonment for not more than thirty years.

In wartime or, in many European countries, in peace, the spy's fate is usually death at dawn. In France he— or she—is lashed to a post facing a firing squad; in Italy, shot in the back; in Germany, guillotined by a gentleman in a silk hat and evening dress. We electrocuted six of the eight saboteurs. Two escaped with prison sentences for helping our authorities, which is common practice. A few countries let off small-fry spies with small penalties.

Big or small, the most disarming enemy agents are, of course, apparent "Americans." They may be persons who (1) seem to have "come into money" suddenly and inexplicably; (2) without apparent reason are always visiting defense areas, antiaircraft stations, shipyards, or other places where military information abounds; and (3) frequent places where soldiers and sailors and officers gather—including the best clubs—and ask them questions about technical matters.

You should report such persons IF you can discover no legitimate reasons for their conduct. But we repeat, it is better to be too suspicious than too naïve. The F.B.I. received an anonymous letter saying that Hans Helmut Gros, a German living near Los Angeles, "played dumb about the American language and stayed out all night." Which seemed pretty slim until investigation showed Gros was an old schoolmate of the notorious Gestapo chief Heydrich who had sent him here to establish a spy ring and prepare to blow up ships and factories. He was just getting started. So, if your case is worth reporting, then report it as quickly as possible, especially if you have aroused suspicion by showing suspicion. "Feel suspicious but don't act it," is a good rule for the volunteer counterespionage agent. Another rule is stressed by J. Edgar Hoover, Director of the F.B.I.: "Do not conduct any investigation on your own initiative. Leave this to trained, experienced, competent, law-enforcement officers."

Just ask yourself, as all good investigators ask themselves: "Am I sure of exactly what I am going to report? What happened? When? Where? To whom? Have I all essential names, addresses, and telephone numbers, including possible additional sources of information or means to check?"

If you cannot answer yes to everything immediately,

perhaps you can quickly fill the gaps. Even if you cannot do that, but still believe you have facts enough to interest the authorities, then report what you have. For Mr. Hoover says: "What may seem insignificant to the inexperienced eye may fit into the scheme of a case already under investigation."

He remembers a complaint that flagrant Nazi propaganda had been distributed by a man traveling on a certain boat with a certain type of automobile bearing a certain license number. A checkup revealed that the man was George Karl Bodenschatz, a wealthy manufacturer of Louisville, Kentucky, who had already been reported for similar actions. The two reports, each incomplete, fitted together and made possible the sentencing of Bodenschatz to seven years in prison for working with Berlin in disseminating Nazi propaganda although not registered with the State Department as a foreign agent. That is required by a very useful law under which propagandists and rumormongers have been and still are being punished.

Hence, government agencies also stress this point: Don't try to estimate the value of your own information. Only trained investigators can do that.

Now, then, you are ready to make your report. Telephone, telegraph, or write, depending on how urgent the matter is. If you think there is danger of the suspect's either taking some immediate hostile action or fleeing, then telephone or telegraph. Ask your telephone Information Operator how to reach the nearest F.B.I. field office, or if none is in your city or town, then the nearest police station or headquarters. If the matter seems less urgent, address your letter, if it concerns exclusively soldiers or the army or army reservations, to:

The War Department
Washington, D.C.

If it concerns sailors or the navy or navy yards, to:

Office of Naval Intelligence
Navy Department
Washington, D.C.

If in doubt, address:

The F.B.I.
Department of Justice
Washington, D.C.

which is the general supervisor and clearinghouse for counterespionage.

After you have made your report, comes another test of your value and sincerity as a volunteer counterespionage agent. For you may never hear another word about it! That is not because the F.B.I. is ungrateful or too busy, but because it is not sound "secret service" to put into the mail anything indicating that you are concerned in such delicate matters. To do so might not only impair your usefulness, but make difficulties for you. But if you receive a caller, whether from the F.B.I. or any other agency, make him show you his credentials, including his badge. If he is a real agent, he will not object. If he is a fake—and there are some—you should report him at once.

And if the person you have reported is not immediately arrested, that does not mean he or she is not being investigated. This takes time, and may, as you read earlier, end in the conclusion that it is wiser to keep the suspect under surveillance than to arrest him. Whatever happens, don't tell anyone that you have reported anything to anybody.

If this sounds like a good deal of advice, and a good deal of work, you will be consoled by remembering (1) that although it comes through the writers, it comes from the best counterespionage authorities in the country, and (2) that you will get your warmest thanks and your richest reward from the best source of all, your own conscience, whenever an American life is saved, or a transport crosses an ocean safely, or a battle is won, or a war —the greatest war in history.

INDEX